The rise and fall of King Solomon

1 KINGS 1 – 11

by James Hughes

the rise and fall of king solomon
the good book guide to 1 kings 1 – 11
© James Hughes/The Good Book Company, 2011. Reprinted 2018.
Series Consultants: Tim Chester, Tim Thornborough,
                    Anne Woodcock, Carl Laferton

The Good Book Company
Tel (UK): 0345-225-0880
Tel (int): + (44) 208-942-0880
Tel: (US): 866 244 2165
Email: admin@thegoodbook.co.uk

Websites
UK: www.thegoodbook.co.uk
N America: www.thegoodbook.com
Australia: www.thegoodbook.com.au
New Zealand: www.thegoodbook.co.nz

Unless indicated, all Scripture references are taken from the HOLY BIBLE, NEW
INTERNATIONAL VERSION. Copyright © 1973, 1978, 1984 International Bible Society.
Used by permission.

ISBN: 9781907377976

Printed in Turkey

CONTENTS

introduction: good book guides

Every Bible-study group is different—yours may take place in a church building, in a home or in a cafe, on a train, over a leisurely mid-morning coffee or squashed into a 30-minute lunch break. Your group may include new Christians, mature Christians, non-Christians, mums and tots, students, businessmen or teens. That's why we've designed these *Good Book Guides* to be flexible for use in many different situations.

Our aim in each session is to uncover the meaning of a passage, and see how it fits into the "big picture" of the Bible. But that can never be the end. We also need to appropriately apply what we have discovered to our lives. Let's take a look at what is included:

⊕ **Talkabout:** Most groups need to "break the ice" at the beginning of a session, and here's the question that will do that. It's designed to get people talking around a subject that will be covered in the course of the Bible study.

⬇ **Investigate:** The Bible text for each session is broken up into manageable chunks, with questions that aim to help you understand what the passage is about. **The Leader's Guide** contains **guidance on questions**, and sometimes ⊻ additional "follow-up" questions.

⊡ **Explore more (optional):** These questions will help you connect what you have learned to other parts of the Bible, so you can begin to fit it all together like a jig-saw; or occasionally look at a part of the passage that's not dealt with in detail in the main study.

➔ **Apply:** As you go through a Bible study, you'll keep coming across **apply** sections. These are questions to get the group discussing what the Bible teaching means in practice for you and your church. ⊡ **Getting personal** is an opportunity for you to think, plan and pray about the changes that you personally may need to make as a result of what you have learned.

⬆ **Pray:** We want to encourage prayer that is rooted in God's word—in line with His concerns, purposes and promises. So each session ends with an opportunity to review the truths and challenges highlighted by the Bible study, and turn them into prayers of request and thanksgiving.

The **Leader's Guide** and introduction provide historical background information, explanations of the Bible texts for each session, ideas for **optional extra** activities, and guidance on how best to help people

Why study 1 Kings 1 – 11?

Solomon can rightly claim to be one of the most famous kings in history. Wealthy and wise, he is credited with writing three of the most influential books ever penned. And the poetic phrases he wrote in Proverbs, Ecclesiastes and Song of Songs about life, love and meaning have entered the English language and are still in common use even today.

These chapters at the start of 1 Kings chart the rise and reign of a man made great by a great God. All of God's promises seem to come together as He establishes what appears to be a "golden age" for the people of Israel. In the whole of the Old Testament after Genesis 3, this is as good as it gets.

But in these chapters are also buried some timebombs which bring the sudden decline and ruin of the king, and his kingdom. Israel under Solomon temporarily hits the heights: but it rapidly plumbs the depths.

This king and his amazing kingdom were only ever a signpost. Through them God points to the time when He will bring a greater reality: a wise King who would not fail and a kingdom which could not be broken—a person and a place which truly is as good as it possibly gets.

The rise of Solomon and his kingdom turn out to be just a shadow of the reality that is to come in Christ. Its peak shows us how wonderful it is when God's people live in God's land under God's King. And its fading splendour reminds us to look forward to the eternal glory of living under great Solomon's greater Son—Jesus Christ.

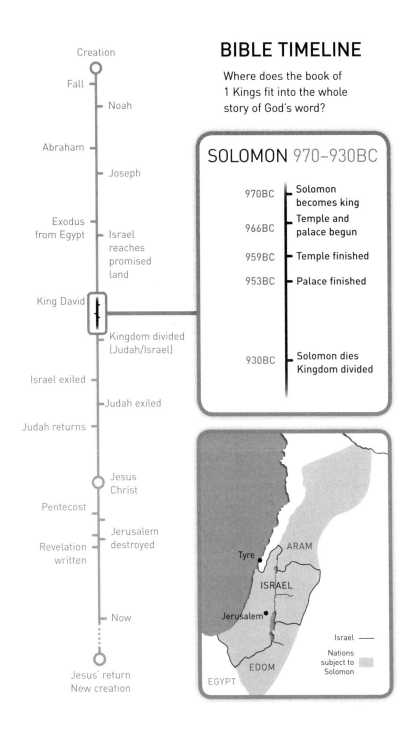

BIBLE TIMELINE

Where does the book of
1 Kings fit into the whole
story of God's word?

Creation

Fall

Noah

Abraham

Joseph

Exodus
from Egypt

Israel
reaches
promised
land

King David

Kingdom divided
(Judah/Israel)

Israel exiled

Judah exiled

Judah returns

Jesus
Christ

Pentecost

Jerusalem
destroyed

Revelation
written

Now

Jesus' return
New creation

SOLOMON 970–930BC

970BC	Solomon becomes king
966BC	Temple and palace begun
959BC	Temple finished
953BC	Palace finished
930BC	Solomon dies Kingdom divided

Tyre

ARAM

ISRAEL

Jerusalem

EDOM

EGYPT

Israel ———

Nations
subject to
Solomon

1

1 Kings 1
SOLOMON THE KING

Who's Who?

It's 970BC in Israel, the land God has given His people to live in. King David is on the throne. He was chosen by God to rule, as a "man after his own heart" (1 Samuel 13 v 14).

God has promised David that his family will continue to rule Israel; that one of them will build a temple in which God will be particularly present, living, among His people; and that one of David's descendants will rule forever (2 Samuel 7 11b-16). God has spoken to David through His prophet, Nathan.

David has a complex family. He has more than eight wives, and dozens of children. His oldest surviving son is Adonijah. One of Adonijah's brothers was Absalom, who rebelled against God a few years before, but was killed in battle (2 Samuel 15 – 18).

One of his other sons is Solomon. He's Adonijah's half-brother, and his mother is Bathsheba. From his birth, God has particularly loved him (2 Samuel 12 v 24-25); and He has promised David that Solomon will succeed him as king (1 Chronicles 22 v 9-10).

David hasn't been a perfect king—but he has been a great one. Now he's old, and approaching death; which is where the book of 1 Kings picks up the story…

⊕ talkabout

1. What are the things in this world—people or events—which make you question how God is at work?

⬇ investigate

❯ Read 1 Kings 1 v 1-27

DICTIONARY

Stone of Zoheleth (v 9): a spring near Jerusalem, the capital of Israel.

Prophet (v 10): someone given a message by God, for an audience chosen by God.

2. What are we told about King David (v 1)?

Adonijah takes advantage of the situation to push himself to the front of the line to succeed his father. He wins widespread, though not total, support from powerful men (v 7). And he shuts some of David's closest circle out (v 10).

3. How does Nathan the prophet react (v 11-14)?

• Read **2 Samuel 12 v 24-25** and **1 Chronicles 22 v 9-10**. Why does Nathan act as he does in 1 Kings 1?

4. How do Bathsheba and Nathan seek to get David to act?

• v 17:

• v 18-19:

• v 20:

• v 21:

• v 24-27:

5. Summarise what this passage tells us about the political situation in Jerusalem towards the end of David's reign.

⤷ apply

6. What do you make of all this jostling for position? How do we see it among God's people today? Is it inevitable? Is it beneficial?

7. What can your church learn from the behaviour of Adonijah, Nathan and Bathsheba (both things to copy, and things to avoid!)?

⊡ getting personal

"What you have said in the dark will be heard in the daylight, and what you have whispered in the ear in the inner rooms will be proclaimed from the roofs" (Luke 12 v 3).

How do you go about getting what you want? At church, at work and in the home, what in your conduct is the all-seeing God pleased with? What would He want you to change?

⊡ explore more

❯ **Read 2 Samuel 7 v 1-16**

What things did God promise King David?

Nathan the prophet delivered God's promise to David in 2 Samuel 7, and is on the scene when the succession crisis erupts in 1 Kings 1.

How do you think his knowledge both of God's promise then, and of David's weakness now, influences his course of action?

⊡ investigate

❯ **Read 1 Kings 1 v 28-53**

8. What does David do (v 28-31)?

> **DICTIONARY**
>
> **Gihon (v 33):** another spring near Jerusalem. Adonijah made his bid for power at a spring, at Zoheleth; David ensures Solomon does likewise, but better!
>
> **Horns of the altar (v 50):** by grabbing these, someone was publicly admitting they had done wrong, and asking for mercy.

9. By verse 40, we have two kings-in-waiting! What is the difference between Adonijah's claim to the throne, and Solomon's?

10. How is Solomon's coronation received by:

• the people (v 39-40?

- Adonijah's allies (v 41-49)?

- Adonijah (v 50-51)?

11. What do verses 51-53 tell us about Solomon?

➔ **apply**

12. God hasn't spoken or directly intervened in the whole of the chapter. But Solomon, the man He loves, and who His chosen King, David, had said should inherit his throne, ends the chapter as king. What do we learn about how God works?

- How does 1 Kings 1 encourage us and challenge us when God's church today is facing a crisis?

getting personal

What situation in your life looks as if God is not in charge?
What will help you to keep trusting that the sovereign God has that
situation under His control?
Resolve to make the most of that help this week.

⬆ **pray**

Praise God...

that He is in control of every situation, and that His purposes cannot be
prevented.

Confess to God...

any ways in which you're trying to resist God's will, or using dubious
methods to get to where you want to be in life.

Ask God...

to give you faith, like Nathan's, in His promises and wisdom—and to help
you take risks when it's necessary to do so to live His way and put His
wishes first.

2
1 Kings 2
SOLOMON'S RULE

The story so far

Despite King David's weakness and Adonijah's rebellion, Solomon has become king of Israel, just as God had promised.

⊕ talkabout

1. How comfortable are you with the subject of God's judgment? How do you feel when it comes to talking about it with others?

⊕ investigate

▶ **Read 1 Kings 2 v 1-12**

2. How should Solomon act as king (v 1-4)?

DICTIONARY

Absalom (v 7): David's son (see *Who's Who?* in Session One).
Jordan (v 8): a river that ran down the centre of Israel.

3. Why does David want Solomon to act against Joab and Shimei (v 5-9)?

⊟ apply

4. David urges Solomon to "walk in [God's] ways" (v 3). Read **Luke 6 v 27-42**. What does Jesus say it means for us to walk in His ways today?

5. Discuss some specific ways you can do this in practice.

⊡ getting personal

In what ways does your life show "the obedience that comes from faith" in Christ (Romans 1 v 5)? In what areas of your life might this be hard to see at the moment?

⊌ investigate

▸ Read 1 Kings 2 v 13-46

6. Why does Adonijah make his request, do you think?

> **DICTIONARY**
>
> **Abishag (v 17):** had looked after the dying King David (1 v 2-4).
> **Ark (v 26):** a rectangular box, covered in gold, with two angels on the lid, kept in Jerusalem. The space between the angels was where God's presence particularly dwelled.

- Why do you think Solomon reacts as he does (v 13-25)?

- Adonijah had "bowed down to King Solomon" (1 v 53). Outwardly, he'd looked loyal. But what was the reality in his heart?

7. What do Solomon's actions against Abiathar the priest tell us about him (v 26-27)?

8. Read **Numbers 35 v 33-34**. Why was Solomon right to want to act against Joab (1 Kings 2 v 28-34)?

9. Why was Shimei executed (v 36-46)?

10. Looking back at the chapter as a whole:

• how was Solomon's throne established?

• what do you make of Solomon's justice?

11. Read **2 Thessalonians 1 v 4-10**. How are King Solomon's actions in 1 Kings 2 pointing us towards King Jesus' actions in the future?

⊡ **explore more**

optional

❯ **Read Romans 12 v 14-21; 2 Corinthians 5 v 20-21**

What is God going to do (Romans 12 v 19)?

In light of that, how should we treat and speak to the enemies of God's King now?

⊟ **apply**

12. Compare Adonijah's words and appearance at the end of ch 1 with what was revealed in ch 2. How does this challenge us as professing Christians?

Solomon establishes his throne through justice and punishing his enemies. And in this he points forwards to Jesus.

13. Do we need to change our view of Jesus?

⊡ getting personal

How much is your everyday life affected by the reality of God's coming judgment?

What impact does that reality have on your gratitude for the cross?

What impact does it need to have on how you interact with your family?

Think of some friends who don't know Jesus as their King. Pray each day for a chance to warn them of Jesus' rule and judgment; and then be ready to take the opportunity when it comes.

⊡ pray

Write your prayers of praise, confession and request based on your reflections in the getting personal box above:

3 1 Kings 3
SOLOMON'S WISDOM

The story so far

Despite King David's weakness and Adonijah's rebellion, Solomon became king of Israel, just as God had promised.

As king of God's people, Solomon established his kingdom by judging and punishing his enemies.

⊕ talkabout

1. What kinds of things make someone wise?

⊥ investigate

❯ Read 1 Kings 3 v 1-15

2. What is the situation in Israel at the start of Solomon's reign (v 1-2)?

DICTIONARY

High places (v 2,3,4): where people from the nations around Israel went to worship their gods—they thought they were closer to them if they were high up.

Statutes (v 3): laws.

Gibeon (v 4-5): the site of the tabernacle (the tent where God could be met). During David's reign it had been separated from the ark (where God's presence was especially present), which was in Jerusalem (v 15).

Discerning (v 9, 12,14): good judgement.

Covenant (v 15): a binding agreement between two parties. God had covenanted to bless Israel as His people, as long as they lived with Him as their God.

3. What is Solomon's response to the situation (v 3-4)?

● What is good, and what is worrying? Why do you think he acted in these ways?

4. God offers Solomon the chance to request what he feels he most needs (v 5). What does the king ask for, and why (v 6-9)?

5. What does God give him (v 10-15)?

6. How does Solomon respond (v 15)? What does he seem to have learned (compare verse 3)?

⊡ explore more

▶ **Read Proverbs 1 v 1-7, 9 v 10**

What is wisdom, and how can we get it?
What is meant by "fear of the LORD" (v 7)?

⊟ apply

7. What have we seen is the way to live that pleases God (v 10, 14)?

• What kind of things do we tend to ask God for, instead of wisdom?

⊡ getting personal

Are you daily asking God to show you how to live and to please Him, as you seek to obey His commands?

It's very easy to listen to other sources of "wisdom". Are there any aspects of your life where you are, or are in danger of, doing this? What would it look like to listen to God's wisdom in those areas?

⊥ investigate

▶ **Read 1 Kings 3 v 16-28**

8. Why is this case such a difficult one (v 16-22)?

9. How does Solomon show his wisdom (v 23-28)?

Solomon's rule has started impressively, and the future seems bright. This humble and wise man seems destined to be the greatest king of God's people. But…

10. Read **Deuteronomy 7 v 1-4.** Why were Israelite men not to marry women who worshipped other "gods"?

- What hint is there in 1 Kings 3 which suggests that Solomon, while great, isn't God's perfect king—and that he's storing up trouble for himself?

⊡ **explore more**

optional

▶ **Read Matthew 7 v 24-29**

Compare verses 28-29 with 1 Kings 3 v 28.

What are the similarities between Solomon and Jesus?

▶ **Read Colossians 2 v 2-3**

What is the difference between Solomon's wisdom and Christ's wisdom?

⊡ apply

11. "All the treasures of wisdom and knowledge" are found in Christ (Colossians 2 v 3). What are the implications of this for anyone now who wants to be truly wise?

⊡ getting personal

God tells us to "let the word of Christ dwell in you richly as you teach and admonish each other with all wisdom" (Colossians 3 v 16).

Are you committed to growing in God's wisdom by reading Christ's words in the Bible? How can you do this more, and how can you better remember what you read?

Do you use your knowledge of Scripture not only to live wisely yourself, but to encourage others in your church? How can you begin to do this more?

Is there any Christian you know who needs gently admonishing about an area of their life where they're not living according to God's wisdom? Would you be willing to listen to a wise admonishment yourself?

⊡ pray

Re-read 1 Kings 3 v 6-9.
Base your prayers of thanksgiving and request on Solomon's prayer here.

4 1 Kings 4 – 5
SOLOMON'S WEALTH

The story so far

Despite King David's weakness and Adonijah's rebellion, Solomon became king of Israel, just as God had promised.

As king of God's people, Solomon established his kingdom by judging and punishing his enemies.

Solomon asked God for wisdom, and God gave him greater wisdom than ever seen before. The king used his God-given wisdom to rule his people well.

⊕ talkabout

1. What kinds of things does a good government do?

⊕ investigate

> Read 1 Kings 4

2. What do the details of Solomon's officials and governors tell us about his kingdom and the way he ruled it (v 1-19)?

3. Read **Genesis 12 v 1-7.** How do God's promises to Abram (who God later renamed Abraham) relate to what is said in 1 Kings 4:

- verses 20-21?

- verses 24-25?

- verse 34?

4. What do the details about provisions tell us about Solomon's court (v 22-23, 26-28)?

5. How did Solomon's God-given wisdom show itself (v 29-34)?

⊡ **explore more**

The picture of "each man under his own vine and fig-tree" (v 25) comes up regularly throughout the Old Testament.

In **Deuteronomy 8 v 8**, God uses vines and fig-trees to help describe the good land He is going to give His people to enjoy under His rule.

▶ Read Jeremiah 5 v 11-19

What's the message of the destruction of the vines and fig trees (v 17)?

▶ Read Zechariah 3 v 9-10

When will God's people again "sit under their vines and fig trees" (see end of v 9)? What is that referring to?

So, what reality do the vines and fig trees point to?

What do these two passages, written after the time of 1 Kings, tell us about Solomon's reign?

⊟ apply

6. Is God's plan for all Christians to enjoy peace and prosperity in this world, just as Solomon did? What does the New Testament teach about this in:

• **Matthew 10 v 34-39?**

• **Philippians 4 v 12-13?**

• **Hebrews 10 v 32-36?**

• What are some of the true riches of God's King (Jesus Christ) and God's people (His followers) today?

The wealth of Solomon's kingdom isn't something we should expect to experience, or strive to gain, as God's people in this world. But wonderfully, all that God's people enjoyed under King Solomon is just a glimpse of what Christians will enjoy under King Jesus in His kingdom!

⊡ getting personal

What fills you with longing, or makes your heart beat faster—worldly wealth, or the riches of God's grace in Christ?

Why not say to yourself each time you long for, or face losing, earthly riches: "You have better and lasting possessions" (Hebrews 10 v 34)?

⊍ investigate

> **Read 1 Kings 5**

7. Why will it be Solomon who builds the temple (v 1-6)?

8. What do these construction details tell us about the temple project (v 13-18)?

• What does this chapter tell us about Solomon's priorities as King?

⊟ apply

9. According to 1 Kings 4 and 5, what makes for good government?

10. How does this passage teach us how to pray for those who have authority:

- in the church?

- in the state (see also **1 Timothy 2 v 1-2**; **Romans 13 v 1-7**)?

⊟ getting personal

How regularly do you pray for your nation's government? Are your prayers mainly a list of what they do wrong, or do you pray positively for them?

1 Timothy 2 and Romans 13 show us how Christians are to live under governments. Are there any specific changes you need to make to your attitudes or actions?

⬆ pray

For your nation...

Praise God for the gift of good government. Praise Him for anything specific about the way your country is governed which you are able to give thanks for.

Pray that His wisdom would guide your governing authorities (whether they acknowledge God's rule or not).

For God's people...

Praise God for the riches of His grace in Christ Jesus, and pray that you will not be tempted away from King Jesus by merely worldly prosperity.

Share and pray about anything that has particularly encouraged or challenged you from what you've seen in God's word in this session.

5 1 Kings 6 – 7
SOLOMON'S BUILDINGS

The story so far

As King of God's people, Solomon established his kingdom by judging and punishing his enemies.

Solomon asked God for wisdom, and God gave him greater wisdom than ever seen before. The King used his God-given wisdom to rule his people well.

Solomon's rule brought peace, prosperity and respect from the nations. Israel was a preview of the even greater blessings King Jesus will bring God's people.

⊕ talkabout

1. How can you tell what someone's priorities are?

    • What does that tell us about what *our* personal priorities really are?

⤓ investigate

❯ Read 1 Kings 6

2. This section is all about the building of the temple, where God will live among His people. Why do you think it begins with mention of the exodus from Egypt (v 1)?

DICTIONARY

Cubit (v 2-6): 0.5 metres/18 inches.
Most Holy Place (v 16): the part of the temple where God was particularly present, so His people could meet with Him and know Him by coming to the temple
Inner sanctuary (v 19-23): the Most Holy Place.
Cherubim (v 23,25): angels.

3. What must Solomon do (v 11-13)?

• Why do you think God reminds him of this as he builds the temple?

4. Why do you think so much gold was used in the temple?

☺ explore more

optional

The design of the temple built by Solomon was based on the design of the tabernacle/tent of meeting, which had been constructed during the time of Moses.

❯ Read Exodus 25 v 8-9 and Hebrews 8 v 1-5

Whose idea was the tabernacle/temple?

What was the purpose of the tabernacle/temple (see Exodus 25 v 8 and Hebrews 8 v 5)?

Why don't Christians have a tabernacle/temple (see Hebrews 8 v 1-2)?

⊡ apply

5. According to the New Testament, what is the equivalent of the temple for God's people (Christians) today?

   • **John 2 v 19-22:**

   • **1 Corinthians 3 v 10-17:**

   • What does this mean for those who want to meet with and know God?

6. Solomon spent a great deal of time and wealth on the temple. How can we as Christians imitate him today?

   • How does this challenge us?

⬇ investigate

7. We hear about Solomon's palace in 7 v 1-12. Fill in the following table and compare the two descriptions:

DICTIONARY

Naphtali (v 14): one of the twelve tribes that made up the nation of Israel.

Detail	Temple	Palace
Time taken to build	6 v 38	7 v 1
Size	6 v 2	7 v 2
Materials used	6 v 20-22	7 v 7
Number of verses given to description		

8. From 7 v 13, we're back to the temple. What were the pillars Solomon had made in v 21 called (use the footnote to see what the names mean)?

• Why do you think these were placed at the entrance to the temple?

9. Scan verses 23-51. Why do you think so much detail is included here?

10. What does this passage teach us about Solomon's priorities?

⮕ apply

11. What are our priorities? How might this passage encourage us to alter them?

⊡ getting personal

If someone lived with you for a week, and could see your diary and your bank balance, where do you think they would place Jesus Christ and His church in a list of your priorities?

Does anything need to change to make the Lord number one on that list?

⬆ pray

Thank God...

- for the Lord Jesus, where God came to earth in all His fullness.
- for the church, where God particularly dwells in His world today.

Go round the group and collect other things from this passage to give thanks for.

Ask God...

- to help you to see clearly what your priorities really are, and for any changes you've been challenged to make.
- to make your church a fit place for Him to dwell in.

6 1 Kings 8
SOLOMON'S PRAYER

The story so far

Solomon asked God for wisdom, and God gave him greater wisdom than ever seen before. The king used his God-given wisdom to rule his people well.

Solomon's rule brought peace, prosperity and respect from the nations. Israel was a preview of the even greater blessings King Jesus will bring God's people.

Solomon worshipped God by using time and wealth to build God's dwelling-place, the temple. But he also spent much time and money on his own palace.

⊕ talkabout

1. What is God like?

⊕ investigate

> **Read 1 Kings 8 v 1-21**

2. What do the contents of the ark, and the events surrounding its coming into the temple, teach us about God (v 9-13)?

DICTIONARY

Tent of meeting (v 4): another name for the tabernacle.
Stone tablets (v 9): on which God had written His law to give to Moses.
Horeb (v 9): another name for Mount Sinai, the mountain where God gave Moses His law.
Cloud (v 10,11): God's presence was often made visible by a cloud (eg: Exodus 13 v 21, Mark 9 v 7).

3. As Solomon speaks to the people, what does he remind them God has done for them (v 14-21)?

> **Read 1 Kings 8 v 22-30**

4. What does Solomon tell God that He has done (v 23-24)?

• What does Solomon therefore ask God to do (v 25-26)?

• How are the two linked (notice the repeated word in v 24, 25, and 26)?

5. If God doesn't live only in the temple, why was it built (v 27-30)?

- Remember that Solomon is praying aloud "in front of the whole assembly of Israel" (v 22). What mistaken thinking are his words guarding them against?

➔ apply

6. What promises of God do we sometimes find hard to trust will really happen?

- Think about where Solomon looked. How can we renew our confidence in God's promises about the present and the future?

7. How should Solomon's prayer shape our prayers?

▣ getting personal

When you pray this week, what one change could you make so that your prayers better reflect Solomon's faith and confidence?

⬇ investigate

❯ Read 1 Kings 8 v 31-53

8. Solomon deals with a number of scenarios in these verses. What are they, and what unites them?

9. What role does the temple play in verses 41-43?

❯ Read 1 Kings 8 v 54-66

10. What does Solomon's last speech ask of God (v 56-60)?

• What is required of the people (v 61)?

11. Jesus is "the image of the invisible God ... God was pleased to have all his fullness dwell in him" (Colossians 1 v 15, 19).
Look back at verse 27. How does this help us see how mind-boggling the truth of Colossians 1 is?

- Jesus is the ultimate place where God's "name" is. How should this affect how we read v 31-53 as Christians?

⊡ explore more

optional

The system of priest and sacrifices in the tabernacle/temple was part of the "old" covenant. Jesus' coming brought a new covenant (Luke 22 v 19-20), in which He is the temple (John 2 v 19-22), high priest (Hebrews 4 v 14) and sacrifice (1 John 4 v 10).

Read the section of Hebrews 9 – 10 listed below, and complete the table to compare the old and new covenants.

Old covenant	New covenant
9 v 7-10: The old covenant could not...	**9 v 11, 24:** The new covenant is better because...
9 v 13: The old covenant could only...	**9 v 12-14:** The new covenant is better because...
10 v 1-4: The old covenant could only...	**9 v 25-28:** The new covenant is better because...

⊡ apply

12. How does 1 Kings 8 shape our thinking on what God is like, and what He has done?

⊡ getting personal

Solomon knew the God who made the heavens could never be small enough to be "boxed in" by a single building. He's much bigger than that!

Does God, in your thinking, ever become smaller than He really is? When do you treat God as though He's less important or powerful than you? When do you find yourself telling God what He should be like, rather than listening to what He says you should be like? Or when do you tell God how He should act in a certain situation, rather than asking Him to act according to His will and love?

The God you can speak to is the God who "even the highest heaven cannot contain" (v 27). What difference will remembering that truth make to your week?

⊡ pray

Praise God...

for the promises given to His people in Christ, which you can be confident will never fail.

Confess...

times when you have failed to trust God's character, or to thank Him for His goodness to you.

Pray for...

yourself and other Christians, that God will turn your hearts to Himself and help you to be fully committed and obedient to Him.

7 1 Kings 9 – 10
SOLOMON AND THE QUEEN

The story so far

Solomon's rule brought peace, prosperity and respect from the nations. Israel was a preview of the even greater blessings King Jesus will bring God's people.

Solomon worshipped God by using time and wealth to build God's dwelling-place, the temple. But he also spent much time and money on his own palace.

Solomon prayed, confident that God would keep on keeping His promises, because He'd always kept His promises in the past.

⊕ talkabout

1. If you were a foreign journalist writing a report about Solomon's Israel, what would you write?

⊕ investigate

> **Read 1 Kings 9 v 1-9**

2. How does God encourage Solomon (v 1-5)?

• What does He warn the king (v 6-9)?

optional

⊡ explore more

❯ Read 1 Kings 9 v 10-28

Solomon is God's chosen king, who has built the LORD's temple. But he's also a king with a kingdom to run, which we get an insight into here.

What do we learn about Solomon's:
* *diplomacy (v 10-14)?*
* *improvement of his territory (v 17-23)?*
* *religious activities (v 25)?*
* *economy (v 26-28)?*

Why does the writer of 1 Kings include these everyday, more mundane details, do you think?

❯ Read 1 Kings 10 v 1-13

3. Why and how does the queen of Sheba come (v 1-2)?

DICTIONARY

Sheba (v 1): a country that was probably in Arabia.
Talent (v 10): about 5½ stone/34 kilograms.

• What does she find (v 3-8)?

4. What does the queen do in response to what she's seen of Israel and its king (v 9-10)? What is she showing about how to respond rightly to God?

5. **Read 1 Kings 8 v 41-43, 59-60.** How is this part of Solomon's prayer answered here?

- God had promised Abram centuries before: "I will make you into a great nation and I will bless you … all peoples on earth will be blessed through you (Genesis 12 v 2, 3). To be blessed is to live as we were made to, enjoying life in God's world under God's rule.
  How are God's promises being fulfilled in Solomon's reign?

→ **apply**

The queen of Sheba came to find out about Israel and its king because of "the report I heard in my own country" (v 6). Read **1 Thessalonians 1 v 6-10.**

6. What "report" should be made about a local church?

• What "report" would your community make about your church?

• What could you do as an individual to make your church's "report" more like the Thessalonians'?

• And collectively?

☺ getting personal

Are you living and speaking in a way that makes faith in the Lord look attractive to those who don't know God? Would your family, friends and colleagues see in your life Spirit-fuelled joy; a rejection of idols; and an excitement about Jesus' return?

Think of one or two practical ways in which the Lord's message could "ring out" in your everyday conversation this week.

☺ explore more

optional

Solomon's kingly wisdom, overwhelmingly splendid as it is, is still only a pointer to the greater kingship and wisdom of Jesus Christ (Matthew 12 v 42).

▶ **Read Romans 10 v 9-13 and Galatians 3 v 8, 13-14, 26-29**

How is King Jesus the ultimate fulfilment of God's promise to Abraham of blessing to all nations?

⊕ investigate

> ❱ **Read 1 Kings 10 v 14-29**

7. How did Solomon show and expand his wealth?

8. 1 Kings 9 v 10 – 10 v 29 shows that Solomon had gifts, wealth, wisdom and influence. What responsibility does he have (look back to 9 v 4-7)?

• How does chapter 10 suggest he is doing with this responsibility?

9. Read **Deuteronomy 17 v 16-17**. What is worrying about 1 Kings 10 v 26-29?

• What does this suggest Solomon is starting to do?

➔ apply

God has given each of His people gifts, wealth, wisdom and influence (though probably not as much as He gave Solomon!).

10. What are our responsibilities when it comes to using these things?

• What are the dangers of having these things?

⊡ getting personal

Do you see God's gifts to you as being for your comfort and enjoyment—or for pointing to Him so that He might get the praise He deserves?

Are there any gifts you have (time, talents, and so on) that you need to begin to use in God's service, rather than your own?

⬆ pray

Thank God for...

Confess to God that...

Ask God for His help with...

8 1 Kings 11
SOLOMON'S FALL

The story so far

Solomon worshipped God by using time and wealth to build God's dwelling-place, the temple. But he also spent much time and money on his own palace.

Solomon prayed, confident that God would keep on keeping His promises, because He'd always kept His promises in the past.

The king's reign, and Old Testament Israel, reaches its high point as the queen of Sheba visits, worships the LORD and gives gifts to His king. God's blessed people are the way God is blessing the world. *But trouble is brewing…*

⊕ talkabout

1. What would you say "idolatry" is? Does it matter?

⊕ investigate

> **Read 1 Kings 11 v 1-13**

2. What did Solomon do (v 1)?

> **DICTIONARY**
>
> **Concubine (v 3):** official live-in mistress.

• Why did that matter (v 2-8)?

3. How does verse 6 sum it up?

• What is shocking about the fact that this is *Solomon* we're reading about?

⊡ **explore more**

> **Read Exodus 34 v 11-16 and Deuteronomy 7 v 1-4**

Why had God said intermarriage was wrong?

optional

4. What do God's words in verses 9-13 tell us about David and Solomon?

• And about God?

⊝ apply

5. Using verses 1-13, how would you now define:
- what idolatry is? Make sure your definition covers idolatry today as well as in Solomon's time.

- why it matters?

6. How do God's commands about marriage to His Old Testament people apply to us as His people today? Read **1 Corinthians 7 v 39** and **2 Corinthians 6 v 14-16.**

- How does 1 Kings 11 show that who we are married to is important?

⊡ getting personal

▶ **Read Revelation 21 v 6-8**

No one is immune from the lure of worshipping something other than God. What things in your life could turn your heart away from the Lord your God? What danger threatens you if you don't seek God's help now to get rid of your idols?

⬇ investigate

❯ Read 1 Kings 11 v 14-43

7. God had given faithful Solomon "rest on every side, and … no adversary" (5 v 4). How is this blessing withdrawn (11 v 14-25)?

8. Look at what God promised in v 11-13. How does He fulfil this (v 26-40)?

- What hope is left for David's line?

9. Verse 43 marks the end of King Solomon's remarkable reign. On the graph below, draw a curve of how things have gone for God's people under Solomon's rule.

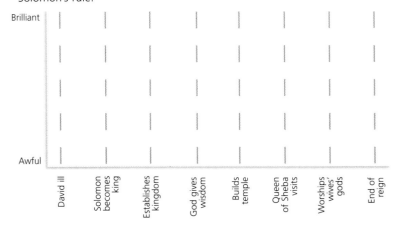

➔ apply

10. How do these verses both challenge and comfort us as we reflect on:
- who God is?

- what humans (even Solomon) are like?

Jesus was born in the family tree of David and Solomon (see Matthew 1 v 1, 6-16).

11. How does the best of Solomon's rule and kingdom leave us aching for the coming of Jesus Christ's rule and kingdom?

- How does the worst of Solomon's rule and kingdom leave us aching too?!

Solomon's kingdom was, in the history of the Old Testament, as good as it got. But it was not as good as it will get. When Christians stand in the Lord's eternal kingdom, then, finally, we will be able to say to each other: "This is as good as it gets: and it's brilliant!"

And so, for now, we cry: "Come, Lord Jesus" (Revelation 22 v 20).

⊡ getting personal

Reflect on the similarities and contrasts between King Solomon and King Jesus. How have these studies helped you to better understand Jesus Christ? How have they prompted you to be excited about His rule and kingdom?

How will this affect your life now?

⊡ pray

Read about the future for God's people under God's King in **Revelation 7 v 15-17**. Use this picture to shape your prayers of adoration, thanksgiving, confession and request.

The rise and fall of King Solomon

1 Kings 1 – 11

LEADER'S GUIDE

Leader's Guide

INTRODUCTION

Leading a Bible study can be a bit like herding cats—everyone has a different idea of what the passage could be about, and a different line of enquiry that they want to pursue. But a good group leader is more than someone who just referees this kind of discussion. You will want to:

- correctly understand and handle the Bible passage. But also…

- encourage and train the people in your group to do this for themselves. Don't fall into the trap of spoon-feeding people by simply passing on the information in the Leader's Guide. Then…

- make sure that no Bible study is finished without everyone knowing how the passage is relevant for them. What changes do you all need to make in the light of the things you have been learning? And finally…

- encourage the group to turn all that has been learned and discussed into prayer.

Your Bible-study group is unique, and you are likely to know better than anyone the capabilities, backgrounds and circumstances of the people you are leading. That's why we've designed these guides with a number of optional features. If they're a quiet bunch, you might want to spend longer on talkabout. If your time is limited, you can choose to skip explore more, or get people to look at these questions at home. Can't get enough of Bible study? Well, some studies have optional extra homework projects. As leader, you can adapt and select the material to the needs of your particular group.

So what's in the Leader's Guide? The main thing that this Leader's Guide will help you to do is to understand the major teaching points in the passage you are studying, and how to apply them. As well as guidance on the questions, the Leader's Guide for each session contains the following important sections:

THE BIG IDEA

One key sentence will give you the main point of the session. This is what you should be aiming to have fixed in people's minds as they leave the Bible study. And it's the point you need to head back towards when the discussion goes off at a tangent.

SUMMARY

An overview of the passage, including plenty of useful historical background information.

OPTIONAL EXTRA

Usually this is an introductory activity that ties in with the main theme of the Bible study, and is designed to "break the ice" at the beginning of a session. Or it may be a "homework project" that people can tackle during the week.

So let's take a look at the various different features of a Good Book Guide:

⊕ talkabout

Each session kicks off with a discussion question, based on the group's opinions or experiences. It's designed to get people talking and thinking in a general way about the main subject of the Bible study.

⊕ investigate

The first thing you and your group need to know is what the Bible passage is about, which is the purpose of these questions. But watch out—people may come up with answers based on their experiences or teaching they have heard in the past, without referring to the passage at all. It's amazing how often we can get through a Bible study without actually looking at the Bible! If you're stuck for an answer, the Leader's Guide contains guidance on questions. These are the answers to direct your group to. This information isn't meant to be read out to people—ideally, you want them to discover these answers from the Bible for themselves. Sometimes there are optional follow-up questions (see ⊗ in guidance on questions) to help you help your group get to the answer.

⊡ explore more

These questions generally point people to other relevant parts of the Bible. They are useful for helping your group to see how the passage fits into the "big picture" of the whole Bible. These sections are OPTIONAL—only use them if you have time. Remember that it's better to finish in good time having really grasped one big thing from the passage, than to try and cram everything in.

⊟ apply

We want to encourage you to spend more time working at application—too often, it is simply tacked on at the end. In the Good Book Guides, apply sections are mixed in with the investigate sections of the study. We hope that people will realise that application is not just an optional extra, but rather, the whole purpose of studying the

Bible. We do Bible study so that our lives can be changed by what we hear from God's word. If you skip the application, the Bible study hasn't achieved its purpose.

These questions draw out practical lessons that we can all learn from the Bible passage. You can review what has been learned so far, and think about practical differences that this should make in our churches and our lives. The group gets the opportunity to talk about what they personally have learned.

⊡ getting personal

These can be done at home, but it is well worth allowing a few moments of quiet reflection during the study for each person to think and pray about specific changes they need to make in their own lives. Why not have a time for reporting back at the beginning of the following session, so that everyone can be encouraged and challenged by one another to make application a priority?

⊡ pray

In Acts 4 v 25-30 the first Christians quoted Psalm 2 as they prayed in response to the persecution of the apostles by the Jewish religious leaders. Today however, it's not as common for Christians to base prayers on the truths of God's word as it once was. As a result, our prayers tend to be weak, superficial and self-centred rather than bold, visionary and God-centred.

The prayer section is based on what has been learned from the Bible passage. How different our prayer times would be if we were genuinely responding to what God has said to us through His word.

1 Kings: the big picture

At face value, the story of 1 Kings 1 – 11 is the story of the rise and fall of a great king. From it, we can take many great lessons about how we should think about leadership, and about the dangers of wealth and power.

GOD'S HISTORY

But to leave it there is to miss out on the big picture. This is not just history. It is God's history. The story of how He chose and rescued a people. The story of how He was preparing to unveil His great plan to save people from all nations and all tribes.

As you work through these studies, you will spend much of your time dealing with the details in each passage, and applying the insight it gives to your lives as you seek to serve Christ today.

But don't miss out on the bigger picture of what is going on. Centuries before, God had promised Abraham that he would be the father of a great people, with a land of their own, who would be a blessing to the whole world, and that He would live among them. Decades before, He had promised King David that His descendant would rule a kingdom that would last forever. God has bound Himself to His people by a sacred covenant.

And the people live under this covenant. This is the faith of Israel—looking to the "golden age" when God will come good on these promises.

As the history of Israel unfolds, we see how the Lord brings about the fulfilment of these promises. Israel becomes a nation with a land. God richly blesses them. Now, under Solomon, God's people live under God's wise king, in God's place, with the temple—the place where God met with and revealed Himself to His people—at its heart.

The high point is the arrival of the queen of Sheba. She represents the people of the pagan world. "All the nations of the world will be blessed through you," God promised Abraham. And here is this exotic pagan queen, who sees the glory of Solomon and Israel, and says, in effect: "What a wonderful thing it is to have the living God as your God".

LOOKING FORWARD

But, of course, this is not the end of the story. While we see a golden age in these chapters, all through there are dark storms on the horizon. And when the come, the decline and fall are catastrophic.

The golden age of Solomon is not what God's people are looking forward to. It is a model, a picture, of what it will be, but God breaks it. And we are left with the questions:

- Where is the truly wise King who will lead God's people?

- Where is the truly safe and prosperous land that God has promised us?

- When will God truly bless all the nations of the world through the children of Abraham?

So as you work through these studies on Solomon, keep looking out for the signs that all is not well. Because these things will point us to God's ultimate fulfilment of His promises in Jesus, the truly wise King; in the new creation, the place of blessing for God's people; and in the gospel, through which God blesses the whole world by offering forgiveness and new life.

1

1 Kings 1
SOLOMON THE KING

THE BIG IDEA
God demonstrates His sovereignty and fulfils His promise, by placing Solomon on Israel's throne despite adverse circumstances.

SUMMARY
1 Kings 1 deals with how Solomon became king. At the start of the chapter we meet King David, who cannot keep warm, let alone rule his nation. As happened earlier in his reign (see the second half of 2 Samuel), one of his sons—this time, Adonijah—tries to fill the power vacuum, but is thwarted when Bathsheba and Nathan intervene to ensure that Solomon becomes king.

Three pieces of background information are crucially important in terms of David's successor. The first is God's promise to David (2 Samuel 7 v 11b-16) to establish David's house (dynasty) for ever, and to have a father-son relationship with the descendant of David who will have this eternal throne. The second is the special status—"loved by the LORD"—God gives Solomon just after his birth (2 Samuel 12 v 24-25.) Both messages were given by Nathan the prophet.

And then the third is God's promise to David that Solomon is the one who will succeed him (1 Chronicles 22 v 9-10).

And so David himself has clearly promised the throne to Solomon (1 v 13, 17).

1 Kings 1 gives us three accounts of the succession of Solomon to the throne: David's instructions to make it happen (v 32-35), the actual deed (v 38-40), and then the news recounted to Adonijah (v 43-48). The first test for the new king is what to do with Adonijah. Solomon shows wisdom—telling Adonijah that he will be judged by his future conduct (v 52-53)—and thus he sets the scene for his reign.

OPTIONAL EXTRA
Construct a quiz about David to provide some background to the story of Solomon. Use multiple-choice options if your group are not very familiar with the Bible. The story of David begins with God's rejection of Saul as king of Israel at the end of 1 Samuel 15 and continues to the end of 2 Samuel. Key events in David's life include: David's anointing (1 Samuel 16), David and Goliath (1 Samuel 17), Saul's attempt to murder David (1 Samuel 18), David and Jonathan (1 Samuel 20), David refusing to kill Saul (1 Samuel 24 and 26), God's promise to David (2 Samuel 7), David's adultery and murder of Uriah (2 Samuel 11), and the birth of Solomon (2 Samuel 12).

GUIDANCE ON QUESTIONS
1. What are the things in this world—people or events—which make you question how God is at work? There will of course be various answers to this question, ranging from the global (war, poverty, injustice) to the personal (illness, bereavement and other life situations). At the heart of this issue is the question of whether/how God is at work when we can't obviously see God at work—a question which we can look at in 1 Kings 1.

2. What are we told about King David (v 1)? David is old and weak, and focused on his own immediate surroundings and situation. His authority is ebbing away.

3. How does Nathan the prophet react (1 v 11-14)? Nathan recognises Adonijah as an opponent. And he believes that the throne has been promised to Solomon. So he approaches Bathsheba, Solomon's mother and one of David's wives, to encourage her to tell the bedridden David what's happened, and appeal to him to intervene in favour of Solomon (v 11-13). He will then come and back her up (v 14).

- **Read 2 Samuel 12 v 24-25 and 1 Chronicles 22 v 9-10. Why does Nathan act as he does?** 2 Sam 12 v 24-25: Solomon is described as "loved" by the LORD, and Nathan is the one who carries that message to David. 2 Chronicles 22 v 9-10: God explicitly told David that Solomon was the one He had chosen to succeed him as king. Since Solomon is the rightful heir, loved by the Lord, Nathan needs to make sure that Solomon becomes king.

⌄

- **What is this teaching us about the part God's people play in bringing God's plans to fulfilment?** We need to get involved! Nathan didn't just sit back to wait for God to sort things out. He took huge risks in order to work towards God's promises coming true. But equally, he doesn't seem to think it's all up to him—God is ultimately in charge.

4. How do Bathsheba and Nathan seek to get David to act? They seek to persuade the king of his need to act based on:
- v 17: David's promise
- v 18-19: Adonijah's actions in trying to seize power
- v 20: on how Israel wants to see David acting
- v 21: on the threat to Bathsheba and Solomon
- v 24-27: Nathan's implication that unless David acts, it will look as if he is happy with what Adonijah is doing

5. Summarise what this passage tells us about the political situation in Jerusalem towards the end of David's reign. David is old and increasingly powerless. The question of the succession has been left open—there has been no public pronouncement despite the promise that Nathan records. Who will be king? In the past Absalom tried and nearly succeeded (2 Samuel). Will Adonijah, who is similar to him, succeed? And then there are the mighty men and the key officials—prophets, priests, military men—who all have a say and a stake in what happens. Who will they support? The situation is fluid and complicated—and precisely the kind of situation which seems to be all of man and very little of God.

6. APPLY: What do you make of all this jostling for position? How do we see it among God's people today? Is it beneficial? Is it inevitable? It's messy, and it's very worldly, and it makes the future of God's kingdom look very uncertain. And it's a situation played out time and time again in God's people today: in individual churches, and in the hierarchy of denominations—give your group the chance to think of particular examples which may spring to mind. Clearly in many ways this kind of intrigue is not beneficial—but notice that Nathan and Bathsheba, who both have God's priorities in mind, do engage in this intrigue. It seems that sometimes it's right for those who care most about God's king and kingdom to use planning and persuasion (though not deceit or disloyalty).

7. APPLY: What can your church learn from the conduct of Adonijah, Nathan and Bathsheba (both things to copy and things to avoid!)? *Adonijah:* We must not seek to grasp power or influence for ourselves, but submit to God's chosen king (then, David; now, Jesus) and look to His command. The approval of powerful figures must not become a substitute for the approval of God.

Nathan and Bathsheba: We must stand up for what we know to be right, according to God's declared will. We must risk our own safety and position when necessary in order to insist that our church lives by God's word. And sometimes that will mean working out how to get our voices heard!

EXPLORE MORE

Read 2 Samuel 7 v 1-16. What things did God promise King David? God's promise to David in 2 Samuel 7 v 1-16 is a hugely important passage in Bible history. God repeats the promises made to Abraham, and adds more. He promises:

- (v 9) to make the name of David great (compare Genesis 12 v 2b)
- (v 10) to provide a home for His people (compare Genesis 17 v 8)
- (v 10-11) to provide rest from their enemies (compare Genesis 22 v 17)
- (v 12-13) to raise up a son of David as successor to David's throne, and to establish his kingdom
- (v 14-15) to have an intimate father—son relationship with David's successor, involving both punishment for wrongdoing and everlasting love
- (v 13, 16) to establish this kingdom for ever

Nathan the prophet delivered God's promise to David in 2 Samuel 7, and is on the scene when the succession crisis erupts in 1 Kings 1. How do you think his knowledge both of God's promise then, and of David's weakness now, influences his course of action? Nathan has witnessed David's decline, and in light of God's promise it must be clear to Nathan that the glory of David's kingdom now depends on David's successor. Nathan is confident to act because God has promised a glorious future for David's dynasty.

8. What does David do (v 28-31)? He acts: he will keep his promise—Solomon will be king after him. Notice how David makes this oath by the LORD who has delivered him. Here he links Solomon's ascension to the throne with God's faithfulness to him in the past. Surely David is reminded at this point of God's promise to establish his house (dynasty) for ever (2 Samuel 7 v 12-13).

9. By verse 40, we have two kings-in-waiting! What is the difference between Adonijah's claim to the throne, and Solomon's? Solomon's ascension has the support of the king (v 35b), and takes place in the proper manner—not acclamation at a feast, but anointing by God's appointed priest (v 33-34), followed by acclamation by the people, and sitting on David's throne (v 35). Notice also that the LORD was not mentioned as Adonijah made his play in v 5-10, whereas He is prayed to in v 31-37. Adonijah's claim is based on might, power and the appearance of religion: Solomon's is based on God's will and the king's will. Solomon is anointed before God and the people. He is truly God's appointed king.

10. How is Solomon's coronation received:
- **by the people (v 39-40)?** With joy and great rejoicing.

- **by Adonijah's allies (v 41-49)?** They are

worried by events outside their control (v 41)—when they hear that Solomon has been made king by David, and that the people are supporting him, they quickly melt away from Adonijah (v 49), who they realise cannot now be successful.

• **by Adonijah (v 50-51)?** He fears Solomon, so he takes hold of the horns of the altar (a visual way of admitting he's done wrong and is asking for mercy).

11. What do verses 51-53 tell us about Solomon? He shows wisdom and mercy: he could kill Adonijah now but chooses not to. But he warns him that his future conduct will be watched (stay tuned!).

12. APPLY: What do we learn about how God works? The events at the beginning of Solomon's reign are murky, and yet God's will prevails. Solomon's coming to power might not look as we would expect for something which comes from God, and yet God works through this situation to place the one He loves on the throne. He is always in charge: His will will be done.

• **How does 1 Kings 1 encourage us and challenge us when God's church today is facing a crisis?** No crisis within the church (and, let's face it, there are many!) is outside God's control. He will work through that crisis to bring about His good purposes and bring glory and recognition to His ultimate King, Jesus. Intrigue and godlessness within the church never prove too much for God!

And so we are challenged to trust God and not despair; and we have no excuse for turning away from God, or compromising, when we are caught up in difficult times. Like Nathan, we must instead do everything we can to encourage and urge the church and its leaders to live by God's revealed will for it. We need to align ourselves with God's will, even when this means risking our own safety or security.

• **What should our attitude be when it looks as if God's purposes are not working out in our own lives?** From countless Bible stories like this one we see that God's will always prevails. Appearances and our interpretation of them are not what they seem, so we should continue to trust God and live for Him. You might like to read James 1 v 2-4.

---

2 1 Kings 2
SOLOMON'S KINGDOM

THE BIG IDEA
Solomon begins his reign by fulfilling the responsibilities of God's king—to be faithful and obedient to God's covenant law, and to eliminate God's enemies—and in so doing he reflects Jesus, God's ultimate King.

SUMMARY
1 Kings 2 deals with how Solomon's kingship was made secure. David was only the second king of Israel, and the transition from Saul to David had been far from smooth. There was no firmly established

principle of hereditary kingship passing from father to son, nor any clear principle for deciding which of David's many sons, if any, should succeed him. Solomon becoming king is very different to Solomon remaining king!

The chapter begins with David's last words (2 v 1-12), charging Solomon first to walk faithfully before the Lord (v 2-4). Whatever wisdom, power or wealth Solomon enjoys, what really matters is how faithful he is to the Lord. His rule will be established by obeying God's covenant law.

Then David gives Solomon instructions about various people, which is where things get tricky for us, as this requires Solomon to deal with (= kill) Joab (v 5-7), and Shimei (v 8-9). After David dies, Solomon upholds justice by executing those who are guilty:

- Adonijah, whose behaviour finally reveals him to be an outright opponent of Solomon;
- Joab, who is guilty of murder;
- Shimei, who continues to show the same contempt for Solomon that he showed towards David.

Solomon's justice, however, is tempered with patience (towards Shimei) and mercy (towards Abiathar). Solomon's kingship is secured through covenant faithfulness, and the elimination of the kingdom's enemies.

The challenge of this passage is how it applies to us. We need to remember that Solomon, as the king over God's people, had a role to implement God's judgments and law which we as individuals do not have—although we recognise the authority of the state to do such things. What we learn here is that God's king must be faithful and obedient to God's covenant law—and must eliminate God's enemies. Solomon here gives us a glimpse of King David's greater son, Jesus Christ, who was supremely faithful and who will one day exercise ultimate judgment after great patience (2 Thessalonians 1 v 6-9).

OPTIONAL EXTRA

(Links with Q1) Select someone to be a judge, and then give everyone else a simple task (eg: draw a picture of the group leader in one minute) for which the judge must decide a winner (the best) and a loser (the worst). Even at this level of a fun activity, it may well be that the "judge" finds it difficult to decide against anyone. Then suggest moving on to "judging" something a bit more difficult: who is best and worst-dressed in your group, or if you meet in someone's home, marks out of 10 for the venue. (Only go ahead with actual "judging" if you are confident that it won't distress anyone.) Discuss how people feel about making judgments in public against other people in the room. How would they feel about making judgments that lead to a negative outcome for the person judged? Perhaps someone in your group has been involved in a disciplinary process at work and (without breaking confidentiality) can share what it was like to sit in judgment on a colleague. What would it be like to sit as a judge in a court where a death sentence could be imposed?

GUIDANCE ON QUESTIONS

1. How comfortable are you with the subject of God's judgment? How do you find talking about it to others? It would be surprising if many people said "very comfortable"! Allow your group to explore how we view God's judgment—and whether or not people talk about it with others. This question is intended to open up the discussion on judgment to frame our examination of 1 Kings 2.

2. How should Solomon act as king (v 1-4)? Obey God's commands.

⊻

- **What words here describe obedience? What does obedience involve?** Notice the emphasis on walking and keeping and observing. Obedience to God's commands involves learning carefully what He requires and taking action to put His commands into practice ie: it's not something we can just drift into or be relaxed about.
- **What will be the consequences of Solomon's obedience?** (1) Obedience will lead to prosperity—not to be thought of simply in financial terms (although financial prosperity does come to Solomon) but in terms of effective action. (2) There will always be someone from David's family on the throne of Israel. In this sense the continuation of David's throne is conditional on the obedience of his successors.

3. Why does David want Solomon to act against Joab and Shimei (v 5-9)? Some people may read these verses merely as David's desire for revenge, particularly against Shimei. However, David wants Solomon to do what he apparently did not feel able to do during his lifetime. There is an unresolved issue of justice here. Joab must be punished for his murderous violence against Abner (2 Samuel 3 v 6-39) and Amasa (2 Samuel 19 v 13; 20 v 6-10). In Shimei's case, Solomon is to carry out God's judgment on Shimei for cursing his king, the Lord's anointed (2 Samuel 16 v 5-14)—even though at the time David did not act against Shimei. (Note: David did not decide Shimei should not face judgement, but only that he should not die (2 Samuel 19 v 21-23).

Solomon honours this decision: he restricts Shimei's movement (1 Kings 2 v 36-38), but it's Shimei's breaking of these terms, ie: rebellion against the king's laws, that means he dies, v 44-46—see Q9.) Solomon, as the king over God's people, had the role of executing God's judgments and law.

4. APPLY: David urges Solomon to "walk in [God's] ways" (v 3). Read Luke 6 v 27-42. What does Jesus say it means for us to walk in His ways today? This is part of Jesus' "Sermon on the Plain", about how to live as part of His kingdom:
- Love, pray for and help practically those who wrong you (v 27-30).
- Give without expecting anything back in return (v 31-35).
- Be merciful as God is (v 36).
- Use God's standards (or measure) when it comes to judging others, condemning actions, forgiving people, and giving generously (v 37-38)
- Seek to follow Jesus, be taught by Him, and becoming like Him (v 39-40)
- Deal with your own sin before helping others with theirs (but do still help them!) (v 41-42).

5. APPLY: Discuss some specific ways you can do this in practice. Encourage your group to think about specific instances where the "rubber hits the road" for them as individual Christians. You might want to prompt them to think about application in the family, at work, and at church.

6. Why does Adonijah make this request, do you think? Abishag was the girl David slept alongside, the last woman he was this close to (1 v 1-4). It seems Adonijah was still wanting to position himself as the heir to David. He feels "all Israel looked to me as their king" (though this was never the case—chapter 1 doesn't tell us the people accepted him, as they did Solomon in v 39-40); he seems to be positioning himself as a powerful alternative to Solomon.

⊻
- **If your group is struggling: Who would Adonijah look like if he married Abishag?** David.
- **Why would Adonijah want people to associate him and David?** Because David had been king, and a very good one—it might prompt people to think of Adonijah as kingly, too.

- **Why do you think Solomon reacts as he does?** He sees Adonijah's request as the start of a new bid for the kingdom, and so sees in Adonijah's actions the evil he'd warned him against in 1 v 52. Verse 22 suggests that, as his older brother and married to David's last companion, Adonijah will be able to take the whole kingdom from him. Solomon had offered Adonijah mercy, but there came a point where his schemes for rebellion meant he would die. That point comes in verse 25.
- **Adonijah had "bowed down to King Solomon" (1 v 53). Outwardly, he'd looked loyal. But what was the reality in his heart?** He was opposed to God's chosen king, resisting his rule, scheming to get into position to replace him—and all the while saying the right things in public, and even acknowledging outwardly that God had given the kingdom to Solomon (v 15). There was a large gap between his words and his heart!

7. What do Solomon's actions against Abiathar the priest tell us about him (v 26-27)? That Solomon is merciful as well as determined to see justice—so Abiathar is

stripped of his office and his power, but not of his life.

8. Read Numbers 35 v 33-34. Why was Solomon right to want to act against Joab (v 28-34)? The word of God to Moses in Numbers 35 is key here. Joab shed innocent blood—and therefore deserved to be executed. David was not able to carry out this sentence during his own reign. Therefore his house, unless it acted against Joab, risked being implicated in Joab's guilt (v 33). Joab's crimes had polluted the land of Israel (Numbers 35 v 33-34). He needed to pay the penalty for his crimes so that there could be atonement.

9. Why was Shimei executed (v 36-46)? Shimei's execution was caused by his breaking the conditions of his restraining order (v 36-37), which had allowed him some freedoms but also placed him under surveillance (a similar situation to that of Adonijah by the end of chapter 1). However, the ultimate reason for his execution was his sin against David (v 44). His conduct thereafter revealed what he thought about Solomon's decrees—that they could be ignored. In other words, he continued to show contempt to Solomon as he had previously done to David, the Lord's anointed.

10. Looking back at the chapter as a whole:
- **how was Solomon's throne established?** Two key developments have led to the establishment of Solomon's throne here—Solomon's obedience, and the elimination of the enemies of the kingdom. It may take some time to tease this out.

• **What do you make of Solomon's justice?** Solomon's actions may look harsh and bloody; and yet we need to see how Solomon was patient with Adonijah (only acting against him when he became a threat to the throne), how he was merciful to Abiathar, how he acted with justice for the sake of the land and David's line against Joab, and how he was again merciful to Shimei, before acting with swift and final justice when that mercy was rejected. It is worth reminding people that we must allow God's verdict on someone's actions to supersede our instinctive reaction. In the case of Solomon here, God's verdict is positive, which we'll see in the following chapters as He lavishes the king with wisdom and wealth.

11. Read 2 Thessalonians 1 v 4-10. How are King Solomon's actions in 1 Kings 2 pointing us towards King Jesus' actions in the future? Those who refuse to obey the gospel (the message that Jesus is God's King, come to establish His kingdom and bring people into it) will be shut out of His kingdom, facing the Lord's punishment for the way they have resisted Him (v 8-10), and treated His people (v 4-6). Jesus' kingdom, in which His people will live with Him (v 10), is established through judgment of its enemies, just as Solomon's was. But that judgment has not yet come. Just as Solomon gave Adonijah the chance to live as part of his kingdom, under his kingship, so God is patient with His enemies (see 2 Peter 3 v 9), giving them an opportunity before Jesus returns to turn to Him and become part of His Son's kingdom.

EXPLORE MORE
What is God going to do (Romans 12 v 19)? God will judge. He is angry at how people treat those who are part of His kingdom (ie: His church)—and He will give people what their actions deserve. That's His job, and not ours! (It may be worth pointing out here that Solomon in 1 Kings 2 is pointing us towards the Lord Jesus and what He does, and is not a model for us to copy—we are not King over God's people!) **In light of that, how should we treat and speak to God's people's enemies now?** We are to bless them (v 14)! It's not our place to judge them or punish them; instead, we're to show them what life is like inside the kingdom, and what our King is like to those who have rejected Him: a forgiving, blessing King who offers undeserved forgiveness. This is to be displayed in how we act towards non-Christians (Romans 12); this is also the message we're to speak to them (2 Corinthians 5 v 21).

12. APPLY: Compare Adonijah's words and appearance at the end of chapter 1 with what was revealed in chapter 2. How does this challenge us as professing Christians today? Adonijah, as we've seen, said the right things and looked as if he'd become a loyal subject: but in his heart he was anything but, as his actions eventually betrayed. Just because we say we are Christians, doesn't mean we are. What matters is the loyalty of our heart: when faced between a choice of obeying King Jesus or advancing ourselves, which do we choose?

13. APPLY: Do we need to change our view of Jesus? What implications does this have for how we teach each other about Jesus; and how we speak to non-Christians about Jesus? Jesus tends to be seen as a friend, a gentle healer and teacher, or as our dying Saviour. Those are all facets of who God the Son is: but we must never forget that He is also the judge of the world, the terrifying bringer of God's wrath and punishment for His enemies. You may find it helpful to read Revelation 1 v 12-18 to help appreciate this picture of the Lord Jesus. Actually, if we remember Christ's power and authority, then we will be able truly to appreciate the fact that we can be friends with such a person, that He stoops to heal and teach us, and that Jesus went to the cross to save us so that we wouldn't have to face His judgment.

The final judgment of Jesus, and His present anger at sin and rebellion against Him, needs to be taught in our churches, including (with gentleness and sensitivity) in our children's groups. It is part of who Jesus is.

So this means we need to speak to non-Christians about Jesus! The judgment of Jesus when He establishes His kingdom will fuel our desire to tell our friends, because we will be longing for them not to face it. And the judgment of Jesus needs to form part of our message to them. No one will understand they need saving unless they understand what they need saving from. But it is easy to leave out this part of the gospel message, because it often proves unpopular.

3 1 Kings 3
SOLOMON'S WISDOM

THE BIG IDEA

As Solomon asks God for wisdom, and then exercises his God-given wisdom, he previews Jesus, God's ultimate King. He also models how Christ's people should seek and use wisdom.

SUMMARY

Solomon is clearly a powerful king: he is able to conduct a marriage alliance with the king of Egypt (v 1). But he also recognises his own inexperience (he is "a little child", v 7), and understands his dependence on God and His kindness, since God is the one who has made Israel a great nation. So early on in his reign Solomon seeks the Lord at Gibeon, and the Lord reveals Himself to him.

God invites Solomon to make a request, and he asks for wisdom. God is pleased to grant him this request, and also promises him the riches and honour which he could have asked for, yet didn't. Immediately we see an example of this God-given wisdom being put to work, when Solomon is presented with an "impossible" case. His wisdom enables him to devise a test which reveals the true mother of the surviving child. Notice the summary of Solomon's wisdom in verse 28 (and compare Matthew 7 v 28-29).

Nevertheless, there is a hint in this passage that even the wisest man on earth will fail to qualify as God's perfect and ultimate ruler. Solomon's alliance with Egypt and marriage to Pharaoh's daughter (v 1) foreshadow his future fall from God's favour (11 v 1-6), when the worthlessness of this alliance will also be revealed (11 v 14-25). A king with greater wisdom is needed.

In this session we focus on understanding Solomon's wisdom, what wisdom is, how we should seek it, and how all wisdom is now found in Christ, God's ultimate King.

OPTIONAL EXTRA

As a light-hearted introduction, you could google "Homer Simpson's words of wisdom" and read out some of these to your group. Or ask people to share words of wisdom that they have found helpful, perhaps from a parent, teacher, famous person or book—even from a fictional character in a novel or film.

GUIDANCE ON QUESTIONS

1. What kinds of things make someone wise? This question is designed to help us reflect on what we think wisdom is. It's a deceptively tricky question! We might talk about being able to make the right decisions in difficult situations, or knowing what people are thinking, or having lots of experience. We might also talk about the kind of life experiences that lead to someone being wise. Take the opportunity to allow people to reflect on what wisdom is.

2. What is the situation in Israel at the start of Solomon's reign (v 1-2)? Solomon is powerful enough to make an alliance with Egypt and marry the Pharaoh's daughter (v 1), and to begin some ambitious building work in his capital (of which we'll hear much more in chapters 5 – 9).

But there is still a sense of things being a work in progress—Solomon has nowhere to house his wife (v 1)! More seriously, because there is no temple, God's people are sacrificing at the high places, copying pagan nations around them and which He had told them to destroy (Numbers 33 v 52). Overall the situation is good: Israel has a good king—but there is work to do.

3. What is Solomon's response to the situation (v 3-4)? He shows that he loves the God of Israel as he walks in the ways of David (v 3). But he also sacrifices and burns incense (a sign of God's presence) at the high places, which is copying the pagan nations around, rather than obeying how God said He should be met with at the tabernacle.

In v 4, Solomon seeks the LORD at the most important "high place", Gibeon, where the tabernacle had been placed by David (see 1 Chronicles 16 v 37-42—the Bible doesn't make clear whether David was right to put the tabernacle at a high place). The ark, which at this point is separate from the tabernacle, and being kept in Jerusalem, and the tabernacle in Gibeon, are therefore the best places to seek God.

• **What is good, and what is worrying? Why do you think he acted in these ways?** Solomon's love for God and desire to follow in the footsteps of his father, who had been a man after God's own heart (1 Samuel 13 v 14), are very encouraging. But the end of verse 3 is a worrying note—the new king does not take a stand against the high places and point people to Jerusalem and Gibeon, the ark and the tabernacle, but instead joins in worshipping at the high places. Perhaps he knew no better (God has not yet given him his amazing wisdom, v 12); perhaps he was not prepared to challenge the people's religion; or perhaps he himself wanted to worship at the high places and never turned decisively away from this way of worshipping, which came from copying those around him and not from God (11 v 7-8 sees Solomon building more high places). It is a worrying hint early in Solomon's reign.

But Solomon commendably ends up going to the tabernacle in Gibeon to offer sacrifices. It's not clear whether the narrator of 1 Kings thinks this is a totally good idea (he simply calls it "the most important high place", v 4). What is clear is that Solomon knows he needs to seek God, and the next few verses show his humility and dependence on the LORD.

4. What does the king ask for, and why (v 6-9)? He asks for wisdom—a discerning heart to distinguish right and wrong (v 9), so that he can rule and govern the people.

⊗

• **How does Solomon show a sense of history (v 6), and why is this important?** Solomon recognises that he is part of God's plan for Israel (compare God's promise to David in 2 Samuel 7 v 12-16) and that he is on the throne because of God's call and kindness.

• **How does Solomon show humility (v 7)?** He refers to himself as "a little child". He is recognising his own inexperience and how he cannot govern well without God's wisdom.

5. What does God give him (v 10-15)? Wisdom (v 12)—and not just any wisdom, but the greatest wisdom of all time. Notice that Solomon's response pleases the Lord— He wants us to ask for wisdom to be able to live His way and care for His people in the role He's given us, rather than prioritising our wealth and reputation (v 13). God also promises Solomon riches and honour, and a long life, but note the condition stated here—long life depends on his continued walk with the Lord (v 14).

6. How does Solomon respond (v 15)? What does he seem to have learned (compare v 3)? He makes sacrifices "before the ark" ie: the place God where is particularly present among His people, and that He had provided for them to make

sacrifices at in order to stay in right relationship with Him despite their sin. He appears, for the moment at least, to have stopped seeking God in the wrong places (the "high places", v 3), and has begun to have the wisdom to relate to God in the way God has commanded.
He also gives a feast—to be able to know God and live His way is something well worth celebrating!

EXPLORE MORE
Read Proverbs 1 v 1-7, 9 v 10. What is wisdom, and how can we get it? Wisdom here means discipline, insight, prudence, doing what is right, guidance, knowledge etc. The key statement here is in verse 7—"The fear of the Lord is the beginning of knowledge. "Knowledge" = "wisdom"; as Proverbs 9 v 10 shows.
What is meant by "fear of the LORD" (v 7)? "Fear" does not mean terror: it means a right awe which shows itself in a life lived aware of God's standards and rule. You might like to point your group to Exodus 20 v 18-20 to show this. Here, the people of Israel are terrified and want to stay away from God, but Moses tells them not to be afraid. Instead, he says, the (proper) fear of God will keep them from sinning. Fear of the Lord, then, means that we seek Him—as Solomon did at Gibeon (v 4)—and we do what He wants.

7. APPLY: What have we seen is the way to live that pleases God (v 10, v 14)? God is pleased when we seek wisdom from Him so that we can live His way and serve His people. And He is pleased when we use that wisdom in how we live, walking in His "ways" by obeying His word (v 14).

- **Read Mark 1 v 15. What is the most basic way we obey God?** Repenting (turning around so we are living with Him as King) and believing the good news (trusting that in Jesus we find everything we need to have eternal life).

- **What sort of things do we tend to ask God for, instead of wisdom?** Probably often exactly the same things as God suggests Solomon could have wanted most—wealth and reputation, or status (v 13). And perhaps health and a long life too (v 14). Encourage your group to think about which of the things we ask God for, and most seek in life, are in fact requests for wealth, honour or health.
  Some suggestions:
  - a larger house.
  - a good school for our children, so they can get a career which is well-paid.
  - promotion at work.
  - recognition of something we've achieved.
  - wanting security and safety (for ourselves and our relatives), rather than for them to serve Christ sacrificially.

- **Why is knowing God and living by His wisdom better than these things?**

8. Why is this case such a difficult one (v 16-22)?
- The two women are prostitutes, and so potentially unreliable witnesses (v 16).
- There are no other witnesses (v 18).
- The "property" involved is of huge value—a child; and he's too young to identify which prostitute he belongs to.
- Both women have a plausible story.

9. How does Solomon show his wisdom (v 23-28)?
- He gets to the heart of the matter—one person's word against another (v 23).
- He sets up an effective and fair test to draw out the real mother (v 24-26).
- He rules decisively (v 27). Notice how his wisdom here is practical—it is given to help him rule.

10. Read Deuteronomy 7 v 1-4. Why were Israelite men not to marry women who worshipped other "gods"? Because they would end up worshipping the gods of their wives, and not treating the LORD as God. (For an example of this happening in reality, see Numbers 25 v 1-3.)

- **What hint is there in 1 Kings 3 which suggests that Solomon isn't God's perfect king, and that he is storing up trouble for himself?** In verse 1 (notably, before he asked God for wisdom) Solomon married the Egyptian Pharaoh's daughter. Egypt was a nation who worshipped other gods (see Joshua 24 v 14). There must be a worry now that Solomon might end up worshipping "gods" other than the one true God, and instead of enjoying God's favour will provoke God's anger, as He warned in Deuteronomy 7 v 4.
  Note: Egyptians (such as Solomon marries in 1 Kings 3 v 1) are not mentioned by name in the list of "out of bounds" spouses in Deuteronomy 7. But given that Israel has just escaped from an Egypt which had defied and resisted God and enslaved His people (1Samuel 6 v 6), and which was a nation which worshipped other gods (Joshua 24 v 14), it seems fair to conclude that an Egyptian woman was someone who God would not want His people (and especially not their king) to marry.

EXPLORE MORE

Compare Matthew 7 v 28-29 with 1 Kings 3 v 28. What are the similarities between Solomon and Jesus? The wise words of both Jesus and Solomon prompt awe or amazement in those who hear, and a recognition that they have a special kind of authority. Solomon's is recognised as God-given, and Jesus' hearers realise that His authority is unlike anyone else's.

Read Colossians 2 v 2-3. What is the difference between Solomon's wisdom and Christ's wisdom? Solomon asked God for wisdom and was given it by God (v 9, 12). And he was still capable of acting unwisely (as v 1 hints and as we'll see more clearly in chapter 11).

Christ Jesus, though, IS wisdom. All of God's wisdom is found in Him, not because He asked God for it, but because He is God. And He never acted unwisely.

11. APPLY: "All the treasures of wisdom and knowledge" are hidden in Christ (Colossians 2 v 3). What are the implications of this for anyone now who wants to be truly wise? No one can become truly wise without becoming a Christian. This fits with what we have already learned about wisdom from Proverbs: wisdom begins with fearing God = seeking Him where He may be found = trusting in Christ, who alone can reconcile us to God, and submitting to His lordship. And, as Christians, to be wise simply means looking to Christ to guide us in all our decisions, opinions and conduct.

---

4 1 Kings 4 – 5
SOLOMON'S WEALTH

THE BIG IDEA

As Solomon rules with God-given wisdom, God blesses Solomon's rule with peace, prosperity and the honour of the nations, previewing the greater blessings of Christ's rule over His people.

SUMMARY

At first glance, 1 Kings chapters 4 and 5 seem to deal with a lot of almost random information, and we might wonder why we need to know some of it. However, as we look more closely at this passage, we see God's blessing on Solomon and on God's people, seen principally in Solomon's wealth, but also in peace and prosperity for the people. In chapter 5,

which again emphasises Solomon's wisdom and prosperity, we begin to move towards the central event of Solomon's reign, the building of the temple.

The first 19 verses of chapter 4 deal with Solomon's officials—overall the impression of these verses is of Solomon's good governance of the realm. A crucially important summary of the state of Israel in verses 20-24 shows God's fulfilment of the promises given to Abraham in Genesis 12 v 1-3 (and amplified in Genesis 15 and 17)— the people are as numerous as the sand on the seashore (v 20) and they are blessed with peace and prosperity (v 20, 23-24). Solomon's name is great: he rules the full extent of the land promised by God (v 21).

Two themes interlock here—Solomon's good government, and God's blessing of His people.

Verses 22-28 give details of Solomon's daily provisions. Despite the size of Solomon's court (v 22-23), he can keep everyone fed without this becoming too much of a burden on the land.

Chapter 5 focuses on Solomon's correspondence with Hiram, which the writer cites as an example of God-given wisdom.

This session deals with the important point of how Christians today should apply the story of Solomon—not directly, which would lead us to look for material prosperity and national peace in this life, but instead by recognising that the wisdom and blessing of Solomon's rule anticipates the greater rule of Christ, who brings His people the riches of the gospel in this world, and then redeemed bodies and a renewed creation in the life to come. We also think about God's sovereignty over the governments of this world, and how Christians reveal their trust in God's sovereignty.

OPTIONAL EXTRA

Ask your group to get into pairs, and come up with five policy changes they would make if they were governing your country. Share answers, noticing any common policies, any contradictory ones, and any pairs who have disagreed between themselves! Ask them what motivated their policy decisions (eg: what would be best for them/their family; what God would want; what would help others less fortunate than them). This will lead you into the talkabout question, and on into the rest of the study.

GUIDANCE ON QUESTIONS
1. What kinds of things does a good government do? Encourage your group not to address this question as "Which political party is better?", nor "What government policies do I disagree with?" but to ask what kind of things we think are important—what should any government care about (without passing judgement on the relative merits of governments over the last 20 years), and how might any government be successful in achieving those things?

2. What do the details of Solomon's officials and governors tell us about his kingship (v 1-19)? Solomon's system of government appears to have been well organised and effective. It comprised a strong central set of advisors (v 2-6), some of whom we have already met, coupled with an effective taxation system (v 7), which supplied the needs of the government without impoverishing the people. Solomon's government, through this system of district government, extended beyond Jerusalem into all of Israel and Judah.

3. Read Genesis 12 v 1-7. How do God's promises to Abram relate to what is said here in 1 Kings 4 (especially v 20-21, 24-25, 34)?
- **v 20-21:** The people of Israel are "as numerous as the sand", and Solomon ruled over other surrounding kingdoms ("a great nation", Genesis 12 v 2); "they ate, they drank and they were happy" (v 20), and they lived in peace and safety (v 25) under Solomon ("I will bless you", Genesis 12 v 2);
- **v 24-25:** Notice the extent of the territory that Solomon ruled over ("to your offspring I will give this land", Genesis 12 v 7)—see map on page 6.
- **v 34:** Other kings throughout the known

world recognised that Solomon had great wisdom, and came to hear it: through the King of Israel, other nations are being "blessed through you" (Genesis 12 v 3). Solomon's reign is the high point for Israel before the coming of Christ—this is the fullest fulfilment of Genesis 12 v 1-3 until Jesus comes as the ultimate blessing for all nations.

4. What do the details about provisions tell us about Solomon's court (v 22-23, 26-28)? Solomon's court was big: there were plenty of mouths to feed. Yet at the same time, notice how the comments on the provisions are linked to the happiness and wellbeing of the average Israelite. Solomon's court was extensive—but not, it would seem, excessive.

5. How did Solomon's wisdom show itself (v 29-34)? It reached into all areas of life, to what we would call the "arts" and "science" (v 32-33), and it impressed and benefited the surrounding nations (v 34).

EXPLORE MORE
Read Jeremiah 5 v 11-19. What's the message of the destruction of the vines and fig trees (v 17)? These verses take us forward from the time of Solomon into the future, when God would judge Israel for their unfaithfulness towards Him with invasion and destruction by a foreign power. The covenant blessings, symbolised by the vines and fig trees (v 17), would be removed.
Read Zechariah 3 v 9-10. When will God's people again "sit under their vines and fig trees" (see end of v 9)? What is that referring to? These verses look even further into the future when God would again restore His covenant blessings to His people. But notice when that would

happen—on a single day when God would remove the sin of His people—the day of Christ's crucifixion (see 2 Corinthians 5 v 21). **So, what reality do the vines and fig trees point to?** The blessings that we receive when we trust in Christ and what He has done for us (Ephesians 1 v 3). **What does all this tell us about Solomon's reign?** Solomon's reign was the high point of political power and prosperity for the Old Testament nation of Israel. But the people of Israel would not be able to sustain the obedience and faithfulness that God requires, and so He would judge Israel with loss of power and destitution. All this pointed to the fact that something greater was needed—something that God in His grace would do by sending Jesus Christ to die for sins, give us His righteousness and pour out on His followers His blessings.

6. APPLY: Is God's plan for all Christians to enjoy peace and prosperity in this world, just as Solomon did? What does the New Testament teach about this? Some people mistakenly view Solomon and his kingdom as a model of how God wants to bless His people in Christ in this world— what is often called the "prosperity gospel".

• **Matthew 10 v 34-39:** Far from promising peaceful lives for His followers, Jesus assures them that even their closest relatives may turn against them. Jesus' followers must be ready to die ie: they may lose their lives but they will certainly have to give up their rights and self-interest. They must first lose their lives for the sake of Christ before they find them.

• **Philippians 4 v 12-13:** Paul's experience was certainly not one of increasing material prosperity. At times he knew what it was to be "in need", "hungry" and "in want". Yet still he was content, not because he had riches but because he had Christ (Philippians 4 v 13).

- **Hebrews 10 v 32-36:** First-century Christians were insulted, imprisoned and impoverished by confiscation of their property. This was not a judgment from God against them for unconfessed sin or lack of faith, but because they stood their ground (v 32) in living for Christ.

- **What are some of the true riches of God's King (Christ) and God's people (true Christians) today?** As we follow Christ we find life (Matthew 10 v 39)—a fulfilling life, and a life that is eternal. We can know contentment now, regardless of circumstances, because we have Christ, through who we can serve God as we keep going to His heavenly kingdom (Philippians 4 v 12-13). And we have a rich reward (Hebrews 10 v 35-36)—all God's promises that we will be His people enjoying His blessings in His land—to look forward to.

7. Why will it be Solomon who builds the temple (v 1-6)? David was a warrior who knew no peace, so did not have the opportunity to build the temple. God has now put David's enemies under his feet, and Solomon benefits from that—he is able to build the temple. For more on this, see 2 Samuel 7.

- **Read Hebrews 2 v 14-15 and John 2 v 19-21. Where, and how, are these two roles—conquering God's enemies and providing a place to meet and know God—ultimately fulfilled?** On the cross, Jesus defeated the power of the devil and death—and in His death and resurrection, He proved that He is the One where God can be met with and known.

8. What do these construction details tell us about the temple project (v 13-18)? Building the temple was a big project! It was very expensive, and required huge amounts of human effort. This involved using Israelite forced labour. This does not appear to have been the same as slavery—more a taxation on time, where Israelites would be required to work for the king 4 months of the year (presumably at a time to fit around harvests). Though later on Solomon's demands on his people would come to be seen as an unfair burden (see 12 v 4), at this stage the people of Israel still seem to be happy (4 v 20) with their life, including with this way of organising labour for the building of the temple.

- **What does this chapter tell us about Solomon's priorities as King?** His great aim was to build the temple for God, as God had promised he would be able to (v 5). It was to this end that he put his diplomatic skills (v 3-12), his administrative skills and his people's work (v 13-18), and all his God-given wisdom (v 12).

9. APPLY: According to 1 Kings 4 and 5, what makes for good government?
- Wise dealings with the people (4 v 20, 25), and with foreign governments (4 v 21, 24; 5 v 2-12).
- Seeking to ensure/maintain peace (4 v 24).
- Taxation imposed fairly and with a purpose, and without burdening the people (4 v 7, 27-28; 5 v 13-16).
- A well-organised "bureaucracy" to oversee key areas of administration (4 v 2-6, 8-19).
- Being willing to help other peoples (4 v 34).
- Recognition of God's provision and blessing when He gives it (5 v 3-5), and making serving Him a priority (5 v 5).

10: APPLY: How does this passage teach us how to pray for those who have authority:

- **in the church?** Since the church today is God's people, much of what we see in Solomon's Israel is what we should wish to see in the church, though bear in mind that Christians look forward to future, not present, wealth (see Q6). Those who God has placed in charge of Bible-teaching churches need our prayer for:
  - wisdom in dealing with and helping church members, and those outside the church.
  - good administration and organisation
  - a willingness to use God-given wisdom to help people

- a recognition that it is God who provides for and blesses His church, and a single-minded focus on serving Him, seeking to build His kingdom and bring Him glory.

- **in the state (see also 1 Timothy 2 v 1-2, Romans 13 v 1-7)?** Christians should pray for their governments along the lines of the answers to Q9. Additionally:
  - 1 Tim 2 v 1-2: that they would govern wisely, and that they would safeguard Christians' freedom to live for Christ and speak for Him.
  - Romans 13 v 1-7: that they would maintain justice (v 4), and discharge that responsibility fairly, so that those who do wrong are punished while those who do right have nothing to fear (v 3).

5 1 Kings 6 – 7
SOLOMON'S BUILDINGS

THE BIG IDEA
Solomon worships God by investing his best resources into building the temple as God specifies. We do the same by prioritising our relationship with Jesus Christ and His people.

SUMMARY
Here in 1 Kings 6 and 7 we come to a section of 1 Kings 1 – 11 that we might find tedious and difficult, because it's hard to see the point of so much detail and description. This session also covers 89 verses of text, which needs to be taken into account when planning this study. It's important not to get bogged down in the detail, but look out for the comments and small insertions along the way that give us insight into what is happening here.

(It may be helpful to provide a picture of what Solomon's temple looked like—google "Solomon's temple" or use a study Bible. See http://www.gods-word-first.org/Images/solomons-temple.gif for a useful plan.)

These chapters cover: the exterior of the temple (6 v 2-10); the interior (6 v 14-38); Solomon's palaces (7 v 1-12); the furnishings for the temple (7 v 13-51).

The work begins 480 years since the exile (6 v 1), reminding us of God's faithfulness to His promises, and of Solomon's continued dependence on God.

Significantly, right in the middle of the building, Solomon receives a word from the Lord (6 v 11-13). God reminds Solomon that continued possession of the promised land

and blessing is not dependent on building the temple, but on walking with the Lord and keeping close to His commands.

There are two things to note about the interior. The first is the gold—lots of it! Some of this stuff would only be seen once a year by the high priest, and most Israelites would never see the inside of the temple. This is not about Solomon's power, but about giving glory to God. The second notable thing is the attention to detail eg: the cherubim (6 v 23-28). Glory is given to God in the meticulous attention to detail here.

The details about the temple are interrupted by an account of the building of Solomon's palaces. The big question is: what is the narrator trying to teach us by putting this here? One view takes this shorter account (12 verses on the palaces; 70+ verses on the temple) as an indication that the palaces were less important than the temple. Another view, emphasising the greater size of the palaces and the longer time given to building them, suggests the narrator is highlighting a shift in Solomon's focus. Is Solomon beginning to be corrupted by his wealth (see Deuteronomy 17 v 17) and moving away from the word of the Lord (6 v 11-13)? Ultimately the answer we choose doesn't make much difference to what we think about Solomon's reign—we know that things are generally positive until chapter 11. But it does help us to think about the question of priorities, and the fact that although wealth is a gift from God (ch. 3), it is also a potential snare.

Finally, the overall emphasis of this chapter is that it should be our priority to worship God in the way He desires (see 6 v 38). The way in which we approach God is vitally important, worthy of our highest attention to His word and the greatest investment of our resources—time, money, energy and passion. So this session both defines what the priority should be for God's people today, and challenges us about whether our priorities are in the right place.

OPTIONAL EXTRA

Find online a "guess the silhouette" quiz—one country-based one is at: http://www.sporcle.com/games/nucleolus101/countries_silhouette.

This activity relates to the fact that the temple, despite all its splendour, is, like the tabernacle on which it was based, only a copy, an outline, of what is in heaven (Hebrews 8 v 5). You might like to play it at the beginning, returning to the point of the exercise at the end—or play it at the end of the session. (See also Explore More.)

Note: Also look at the Optional Extra activity for next session (p 80) as this may need to be prepared ahead of time.

GUIDANCE ON QUESTIONS

1. How can you tell what someone's priorities are? Priorities are revealed by what we spend our time, our money and our energy on. It's not always a straightforward equation, but we can usually see a pattern emerging over time. Many people have to work to raise money to buy food and shelter—even in our society a significant (and rising!) amount of money goes there. That doesn't mean what they care about most is work and food (although it might!). But when someone has spare time, a little spare money or some spare energy, what do they do with it?

• **What does that tell us about what our priorities really are?** If this is how we discern someone else's priorities, it is also the way we discover what our priorities really are—and they may be different to what we think they are, or know they should be!

We will come back to this question at the end of the session, so treat it as a discussion starter, rather than an opportunity to reach a firm and final conclusion.

2. This section is all about the building of the temple. Why do you think it begins with mention of the exodus from Egypt (v 1)? In some ways, the adventure that began with God rescuing His people from slavery in Egypt (Exodus 12 – 15) finds its end in 1 Kings 6 – 8. God had promised to give His people a good land (Exodus 3 v 8) where He would live among them and be their God (Exodus 6 v 7, 25 v 22). In building a permanent temple in the capital of that land, where God will dwell among the people, Solomon is in some ways writing the last chapter of that 480-year-long story—or rather, God is, just as He began it through Moses.

3. What must Solomon do (v 11-13)? Keep God's word—His decrees, commands and regulations. As Solomon and the people do this, the Lord will live among them.

• **Why do you think God reminds him of this as he builds the temple?** God's promise to bless Solomon and his descendants, and God's people, is dependent on obedience. Having a magnificent temple in Jerusalem is no guarantee that God will bless Israel—what matters above all is obedience to His covenant.

In the coming of Christ, God keeps His promises because of His obedience—we are saved because of His obedience, not ours, though we must now seek to obey Him; see Hebrews 5 v 7-9.

4. Why do you think so much gold was used in the temple? The gold—along with other precious metals, and the precious wood from Lebanon (see chapter 5)—was used to show that this was a place of surpassing value. God's "house" deserved to have no expense spared. Of all the things Solomon could have spent his vast wealth on, the temple was the most important.

EXPLORE MORE
Whose idea was the tabernacle/temple? God's.
What was the purpose of the tabernacle/temple (see Exodus 25 v 8 and 8 v 5)? To create a sanctuary for God's presence among His people (Exodus 25 v 8). But the New Testament adds that the tabernacle and what happened inside it was a copy and shadow of heaven (Hebrews 8 v 5).
Why don't Christians have a tabernacle/temple (see Hebrews 8 v 1-2)? Because Jesus Christ is our ultimate high priest, serving in the ultimate sanctuary—heaven.

5. APPLY: According to the New Testament, what is the equivalent of the temple for God's people (Christians) today?
• **John 2 v 19-22:** Jesus referred to His own body as the "temple".
• **1 Corinthians 3 v 10-17:** In this passage Paul talks about the work of building God's church on the foundation of Jesus Christ (v 11), and in verse 16 he addresses the Corinthian Christians as God's temple. The "you"s in v 16 are plural.
Note: These two references are not contradictory, since there is an intimate connection between Christ and His church, which is seen most clearly in the New Testament when the metaphor is changed to that of head and body (eg: Ephesians 4

v 15-16). In the Old Testament the temple was the place where sacrifices were offered so God's people could be forgiven and made right with God, and where that reconciliation was announced. Today, forgiveness and righteousness are found in Jesus' sacrifice: and the church is the place where that reconciliation is announced.

- **What does this mean for those who want to meet with and know God?** Those who are seeking God will not find Him except through the message about Jesus Christ preached, attested and lived out by the church.

6. APPLY: Solomon spent a great deal of time and wealth on the temple. How can we as Christians imitate him today? Since the "temple" now is Jesus and His church, it's by spending our time and wealth on serving Christ and His people.

- **How does this challenge us?** Is this our priority in life? The challenge will be different for different people: for some it may be "keep going in serving the church", for others it may be a case of rearranging priorities.

7. We hear about Solomon's palace in 7 v 1-12. Fill in the following table and compare the two descriptions:

Detail	Temple	Palace
Time taken to build	6 v 38 7 years	7 v 1 13 years
Size	6 v 2 60x20x30 cubits (plus outbuildings	7 v 2 100x50x30 cubits (plus other buildings)
Materials used	6 v 20-22 Gold	7 v 7 Cedar

Detail	Temple	Palace
No. of v's given to description	76 (plus preparations in chapter 5)	12

- **Which building is more impressive?** Two possible answers here (as in Q10!). The temple, in that it is described first, and described in more detail, and has more precious materials used. But the palace, in that it's bigger, and took longer to build.

8. From verse 13 we're back to the temple. What were the pillars Solomon had made in v 21 called (use the footnotes to see what these names mean)? Jakin = "he establishes"; "Boaz" = "in him is strength".

- **Why do you think these were placed at the entrance to the temple?** Probably as a visible witness to who God is for His people. "He establishes" reminds the Israelites that it is God who established David (see 2 Samuel 7), and who continues to establish and secure the throne of David's descendants. "In him is strength" is a reminder that the king and the people, whatever the external situation might seem to indicate, must rely on the LORD for strength.

9. Scan verses 23-51. Why do you think so much detail is included here? Several possible, and good, answers might be given:
- It is important to worship God in the way which He has chosen, to the last detail. For the Israelites this meant the temple and the sacrificial system. For us it means coming to Christ as Saviour and Lord, and trusting in Him.
- A reminder of the expertise, time, wealth

and effort that went in to building it.
- Parts of the temple could be seen only by priests—these details were a record of the wonders inside the temple.

10. What does this passage teach us about Solomon's priorities?

- **(If your group is struggling) Which was more important to Solomon: the temple or the palace?**

This depends on how we read 7 v 1-12. So what can we say about Solomon's priorities?
- He built the temple, using the best materials and craftsmen and with great attention to detail.
- His palace took nearly twice as long to build and was larger (7 v 1).
- He built the temple as a fitting place in which to worship God.

In some ways it seems God's temple was his priority; but there is a hint that his own palace was a competing priority. It doesn't matter if the group disagree, as long as people disagree based on what the text says, not just expressing a preference. Even if Solomon's priorities remain a little unclear, this question will lead us to application—because what is clear is that Solomon's priority should have been the temple.

11. APPLY: What are our priorities? How might this passage encourage us to alter them? Revisit Q1—when we have free time, a little spare money or some spare energy, what do we do with it? Then review what this passage teaches us. For example:
- The importance of regularly examining our own priorities, to see if they are right before the Lord, and watching out for other things that might take precedence.
- The importance of giving our best to worshipping God—which for us means prioritising our relationship with Jesus and His people (spending time with God daily; meeting with the church regularly and frequently; listening to, learning and growing in the gospel etc). When it comes to how we use our time, energy and money, do we give of our best to the Lord's work?

1 Kings 8
SOLOMON'S PRAYER

THE BIG IDEA
Solomon prays confidently to God because he recognises God's holiness and His promise-keeping faithfulness; similarly, Christians come confidently to God in Christ, trusting in all He has done for us.

SUMMARY
Dale Ralph Davis helpfully outlines the structure of this passage in this way:

Celebration and sacrifice: v 1-13
  Blessing Israel and Yahweh: v 14-21
    Solomon's prayer of dedication: v 22-53
  Blessing Israel and Yahweh: v 54-61
Celebration and sacrifice: v 62-66

This structure emphasises the middle section—Solomon's prayer. Overall, this chapter emphasises God's character—who He is, and what He has done.

Verses 1-13: the temple building is finished. But without the "ark of the Lord"—the symbol of God's presence with His people—the temple is a white (or gold) elephant. So Solomon brings the ark to the temple (containing the stone tablets—v 9), which reminds us that God's relationship with His people is based on the covenant He made at Sinai (Exodus 19 – 20).

The glory of the Lord fills the temple—the priests cannot approach—demonstrating that the God who speaks and makes promises to His people is also a holy God—He must be approached in the right way.

Solomon's prayer (v 22-53) is central to the theology of 1 Kings, and emphasises God's promise-keeping faithfulness. Solomon knows the temple cannot contain God, yet he also knows that the temple is the place in which God chooses to reveal Himself to His people. So he can pray with confidence.

Solomon's prayer appeals to God's justice (v 31-32), and vindication (v 44-45), but most of all to God's mercy (v 33-34, 35-36, 37-40, 46-51). Solomon understands that God will discipline His people, but will be merciful to those who repent and turn to Him. Similarly, Solomon's opening and closing addresses (v 15-21, 56-61) show his faith in the God who has acted, and trust that He will act again.

This session focuses our attention on what God is like: He makes and keeps His promises; He is merciful and forgives those who repent and turn back to him; and He delights to give His people good things. It's because Solomon knows what God is like that he can approach God in prayer with confidence. The session challenges us to think about what the coming of Christ has

added to our understanding of God and what will help us to pray confidently to God.

OPTIONAL EXTRA

Give your group a flavour of what people think God is like by asking a range of people that question (eg: your neighbours, at a party, at the local youth group, on the street). Or google "What is God like?" where you will eventually find a YouTube clip of man-on-the-street interviews shot in San Diego. Get your group to discuss which views (or non-views!) are most widespread among their friends/colleagues, and which are most like their own view of God before they encountered the Christian message. You could also ask how they think the various views affect the way that people pray, or don't bother to pray.

Note: Also look at the Optional Extra activity for next session (p 84) as this needs to be prepared ahead of time.

GUIDANCE ON QUESTIONS

1. What is God like? Get people considering what it is they actually think about God, and how they would sum up what He is like. If the answers focus only on Jesus, encourage them to also think about God the Father. Having looked at who God is in the passage, Q2 and Q11 bring us back to this question.

2. What do the contents of the ark, and the events surrounding its coming into the temple, teach us about who God is (v 9-13)? The two tablets (v 9) contained God's words, His law, given to Moses. God is the God who speaks, and we know Him through His words. God is also a God of covenant (v 9), who graciously binds Himself to His people, promising to bless them (see Genesis 12 v 1-7). God is a God who dwells among His people (v 10-13). And God is a glorious and holy God, who is not like us and who is hugely powerful (v 10-11).

3. As Solomon speaks to the people, what does he remind them God has done for them (v 14-21)?
- He keeps His promises (v 15).
- He brought them out of Egypt (v 16).
- He chose a king to rule them, David (v 16).
- He kept His promise to David, that Solomon will build a temple for His "Name", to dwell in (v 18-20). By "Name" God means the way He can be known and related to. So the temple is the place where God can be known and met with.
- At the heart of Israel is still the covenant God has made with Israel (v 21), the implication being that God has remained faithful to His people.

4. What does Solomon tell God that He has done? (v 23-24)? Kept His promises.

- **What does Solomon therefore ask God to do (v 25-26)?** Keep keeping His promises!

- **How are the two linked?** It's because God has kept His promises in Israel's history that Solomon confidently asks God to fulfil His promises in the present. Solomon's prayer shows that he trusts God to do what He said, because God has proved that He always does what He says. But notice that God's people are still to ask God to keep on keeping His promises, as a sign that they trust in and depend on Him.

☒

- **What does this teach us about prayer?** Prayer isn't about informing God of our needs—He already knows about them. It's about us exercising trust in Him, based on our knowledge of His character.

As we put trust in Him, we learn more of His faithfulness and our trust grows. So prayer is for our benefit rather than God's.

5. If God doesn't live only in the temple, why was it built (v 27-30)? It was the place where God particularly met with His people. The whole people were to gather at certain times to come before the Lord together, and the temple was the place where sacrifices were offered for sin. Solomon's emphasis falls on prayer: the temple was the place where God's people would especially come to seek Him. The temple showed that sinful people could approach the holy God, but only in the way in which God commanded. The temple didn't constrain or limit God's presence; but it was a place of God's presence, where humanity could meet and know Him.

- **Remember that Solomon is praying aloud "in front of the whole assembly of Israel" (v 22). What mistaken thinking are his words in v 27-30 guarding them against?** That God can be limited, or thought of as living in one particular place. It would have been easy for God to become small in people's minds if they thought He simply lived "up the road". Israel may even have felt that God needed them to build Him a house to live in, and needed them to provide Him with sacrifices (a pagan approach to relating to the divine). This is a New Testament concern, too: see Acts 17 v 24-25.

☒

- **What opposite error do we also need to avoid?** Thinking God is so "other" and distant that humans cannot approach Him at all—that the gap between God and man is so wide there is no way for us to approach Him, know Him or relate to Him.

6. APPLY: What promises of God do we sometimes find hard to trust will really happen? Encourage your group to be honest and open. It may be the promise that He will return and remake this world; or that He is always working for the good of His people (Romans 8 v 28); or that He is changing us through His Spirit; or something else.

• **Think about where Solomon looked. How can we renew our confidence in God's promises about the present and the future?** Solomon is confident that God is doing, and will do, what He has promised, because he looks at His promise-keeping work in the past. We should look back at what God has done in history to renew our trust in what He's doing now. We can look at how He kept His promises to Israel; we can look at how He has worked in our own lives; most of all, though, we must look at the historical fact of the cross and resurrection, and what God has done for us in Christ.

7. APPLY: How should Solomon's prayer shape our prayers? Our prayers should:
• tell God who He is and what He's done, as a way of praising Him (v 23-24).
• ask God to keep on keeping His promises, and ask confidently (v 25-26).
• confidently ask for forgiveness, knowing that God hears our confession (v 30).

8. Solomon deals with a number of scenarios in v 31-53. What are they and what unites them? Solomon deals with oaths (v 31-32); military defeat (v 33-34); drought (v 35-36); famine and plague and invasion (v 37-40); foreigners (v 41-43); military campaigns (v 44-45); and national apostasy leading to exile (v 46-51)—things that are mentioned in Leviticus 26 and Deuteronomy 28. With the possible exception of oaths, all these scenarios deal with God's grace—His mercy upon a people who have turned away from Him, yet who are repentant—His mercy to His people in giving them military victory, and His mercy on those who are not His people (foreigners). The emphasis here is on God's covenant faithfulness and mercy, on what He will do for His people (rather than what they do for Him).

9. What role does the temple play in v 41-43? This question is here to tease out the fact that the temple was never intended to be solely for the benefit of the Israelites. It was to function as a beacon, to draw people of other nations into joining God's people.

⌄

• **What does this remind us is the role of our church?** The church is now the place where people can meet with and know God, as it offers people Christ in its life and teaching. Your church is not for the benefit of its members only; it's to be a beacon to those who don't know God.

10. What does Solomon's final speech ask of God (v 56-60)? Solomon asks God to continue to look after His people (v 57)—which means to be with them, and to draw them to Himself (v 58), so that God's people might be upheld ("guaranteed justice", The Message) (v 59), and those of other nations might come to know that the LORD is God (v 60).

• **What is required of the people (v 61)?** The people must be committed to obedience to the Lord.
Note: Covenant obedience, which Solomon is talking about in v 61, does not mean perfect obedience (or no one would be part of God's people!). It means

obedience to God's covenant: that is, a desire to obey His commands, and a commitment to living as part of His people, including repenting and making sacrifice as He desires when His commands have not been kept.

11. Jesus is "the image of the invisible God … God was pleased to have all his fullness dwell in him" (Colossians 1 v 15, 19). How does v 27 help us to see how mind-boggling this truth is? In Jesus, we see the invisible God. In the person of Jesus dwelled all the fullness of the infinite, uncontainable God. God is not constrained by the human form of Jesus: but all of God was in the man Jesus, God the Son on earth. Wow!

• **Jesus is the ultimate place where God's "name" is. How should this affect how we read v 31-53 as Christians?** It's in Jesus that we find justice (v 32); rescue and restoration from self-imposed difficulties (v 33-34); discipline and blessing (v 35-40); an invitation to all peoples to know God (v 43); strength for God's people (v 44-45); and the ultimate rescue from the ultimate exile, the offer of life in heaven instead of hell, for anyone who repents and looks to Him (v 46-51). Again: wow!

EXPLORE MORE
Read the section of Hebrews 9 – 10 below, and complete the table to compare the old and new covenants.
9 v 7-9: The OC could not… open the way into the Most Holy Place (v 8) or clear the worshipper's conscience (v 9).
9 v 11, 24: The NC is better because… Christ is our high priest in heaven itself.

9 v 10, 13: The OC could only… make people outwardly or ceremonially clean.

9 v 12-14: The NC is better because… the sacrifice offered is Christ's own blood, which is able to cleanse our consciences.
10 v 1-4: The OC could only… point to the good things that were coming (v 1); and could only remind people of their sin (v 3) but not take away their sin (v 4).
9 v 25-28: The NC is better because… Christ's sacrifice is once for all, and able to do away with sin.

12. APPLY: How does 1 Kings 8 shape our thinking on what God is like, and what He has done? This returns to where the study started in Q1.
• God is the God who made everything and is bigger than any category we can come up with (v 27).
• Yet He is the God who dwells with and among His people (v 10-11).
• He makes promises and keeps them (v 15, 20, 24, 53, 56).
• God is merciful—He forgives those who repent and turn back to Him (v 33-34, 35-36, 37-40, 46-50).
• And God delights to give His people good things—a king on the throne (v 25), answers to prayer (v 30, 42-43), justice (v 32, 39-40), the promised land (v 34), teaching needed for right living, and rain needed for healthy crops (v 36) and so on.

1 Kings 9 –10
SOLOMON AND THE QUEEN

THE BIG IDEA

Solomon is blessed with wealth and wisdom, and has the responsibility of using these things to serve God with them, to be part of God's plans for His world.

SUMMARY

This section of 1 Kings splits, into four sections. Chapter 9 first deals with the finishing of the temple and Solomon's second encounter with God (9 v 1-9); then with the financial and other implications of the temple project (9 v 10-28). Chapter 10 gives an account of the visit of the queen of Sheba (10 v 1-13), before a final summary of Solomon's wealth and power (10 v 14-29).

God appears to Solomon for only the second time in 20 years, and again promises to remain faithful to His promises, but He also commands Solomon and his descendants to remain faithful to Him.

In the next section (9 v 10-28) we see Solomon doing what kings do, and doing it well.

In chapter 10 the queen of Sheba comes to see for herself the wealth and wisdom of Solomon that she has heard about. She sets out to impress Solomon (v 2), but ends up overwhelmed by his greatness (v 5), and rightly attributes this to God's blessing (v 9)—compare how the Jews of Jesus' day knew more than the queen of Sheba, and yet rejected one greater than Solomon (Matthew 12 v 42).

The final summary of Solomon's wealth in chapter 10 is the last positive thing the narrator will have to say about Solomon before things go wrong in chapter 11, but here Solomon's extensive wealth is related to his God-given wisdom (v 23-25), and outlined in very positive terms.

These chapters have a twin theme. The first is the blessing Solomon's Israel brings to the nations, due to the "report" they are hearing about what life under his rule is like. The second concerns his great gifts, and how he will use them. The first is a challenge for the local church; the second a challenge for the individual Christian.

OPTIONAL EXTRA

In the week before this session, provide the people in your group with resources and an instruction to use them to benefit the group in some way during this session. The easiest option is to give differing amounts of money—ranging from, say, 50p to £10 (or 50 cents to $10)—in sealed envelopes (so people can't compare what they have received), which they can use to buy drinks, snacks, flowers, better mugs or pens, a CD or anything else they think would be beneficial to everyone.

At the beginning of the session, get people to write down on a slip of paper how much they were given, and what they used it for (including if they forgot!). Write it up on a large sheet (anonymously, so that no one is singled out or embarrassed). Then read out Luke 19 v 11-27. At the end you could ask people to vote for the person (not themselves of course) who they think made best use of the money that they were given.

This activity relates to the issue of our responsibility to use our gifts from God in His service.

GUIDANCE ON QUESTIONS

1. If you were a foreign journalist writing a report about Solomon's Israel, what would you write? This provides a useful recap of what the group has seen; but it also gets people thinking about how an outsider would report what's happening in Israel under Solomon—the kind of report the Queen of Sheba hears (10 v 1, 6)—and how an outsider would report what's happening in your church (so this question is worth referring back to as you answer Q6).

2. How does God encourage Solomon (v 1-5)? He speaks to him directly for a second time (v 2). This direct speech from God is comparatively rare in the Bible, so Solomon is privileged to receive God's word twice. And He reminds Solomon of the wonder of having the temple, where God will always be found (v 3), and the privilege of being the one who has built it.

• **What does He warn the king (v 4-9)?** Solomon must continue to follow the LORD (v 4-5). In particular, Solomon is warned about the consequences of turning away from Him (v 6), not just for the king but also for the people (v 7). The temple won't save them—in fact, it will become just another reason to mock the Israelites, and a further example of why they will have been cut off by God (v 7-9). Solomon, and the people, must continue to walk before the Lord.

EXPLORE MORE
What do we learn about Solomon's:
• **diplomacy (v 10-14)?** Not everything was always plain sailing! But notice that Solomon didn't fall for what seems like a plan by Hiram to get some better territory.
• **improvement of his territory (v 17-23)?** He was committed to continuing to

improve Israel through his building work (though some of it was for his own possessions, v 19b).

Note: The point about the conscripted labour here is not that Solomon had such a workforce, but that he did not use fellow Israelites in it.

• **religious activities (v 25)?** He continued to "fulfil the temple obligations". Solomon was committed to worshipping God in the way God had commanded.
• **economy (v 26-28)?** His wealth, and his nation's wealth, continued to increase, as Solomon wisely used his nation's resources in partnership with Hiram's—his men, Solomon's ships—to make more and more money.

Why does the writer of 1 Kings include these everyday, more mundane details, do you think? Life, even for a king, is not always the excitement of temple-building! Solomon was a real king, who had to apply his God-given wisdom in all kinds of different areas of life. It's a reminder to us that we're to try to live for God Monday to Saturday, as well as at church on a Sunday—the everyday details of our lives matter to God.

3. Why and how does the queen of Sheba come (v 1-2)? Because she's heard a report about Solomon and his nation. She comes to see if what she's heard is true. She seems to want to test him (v 1); but she also has much that she wants to get wisdom on (v 2). How often this is the case with those coming into contact with God's people!

• **What does she find (v 3-8)?**
  • The king is wise enough to answer all her questions (v 3)
  • The wealth and wisdom by which Solomon builds, provides and rules is overwhelming (v 5).

- The reality of Solomon and Israel is even better than she'd heard (v 7).
- The people living under Solomon's rule are hugely "happy" (v 8).

4. What does the queen do in response to what she's seen of Israel and its king (v 9-10)? What is she showing about how to respond rightly to God?
- She praises God for the king He's given Israel (v 9). Notice that she recognises God's love for His people, which has prompted Him to bless them with a king who rules them justly and rightly.
- She gives the king gifts never seen before or since (v 10)—that is, she shows her praise for God by giving the king of God's people the best she has to offer. So to respond rightly to God, we must give all we have to His King—ultimately, to Jesus.

⊻

- **(If the group is struggling with the second part of the question) How does what the queen *does* in verse 10 show that she means what she *says* in verse 9?**
- **To worship God rightly, who do you give the best of what you have to?** His chosen king.
- **What would that look like today?** Giving your life to Jesus.

5. Read 1 Kings 8 v 41-43, 59-60. How is this part of Solomon's prayer answered here? His prayer looked forward to the time when those of other nations would come to Israel, and be blessed by God because of the temple. Here, we see the temple is part of what attracts the queen (v 5). The point here is this: God's people living responsibly before God attract others who come to know God, or at least know of God, as a result.

● God had promised Abram: "I will make you into a great nation and I will bless you … all peoples on earth will be blessed through you" (Genesis 12 v 2, 3) … How are God's promises being fulfilled in Solomon's reign?
- "I will make you into a great nation"— the queen's momentous visit is the highest proof that God has made the descendants of Abraham into a great nation.
- "I will bless those who bless you"—the queen first blesses Solomon (v 6-10) and then is blessed by him (v 13).
- "All peoples on earth will be blessed through you"—a foreign, and presumably pagan, queen ends up celebrating the goodness of God because of her encounter with Solomon.

6. The queen of Sheba came to find out about Israel and its king because of "the report I heard in my own country." Read 1 Thessalonians 1 v 6-10. What "report" should be made about a local church?
- v 6—lives that are Christlike. Encourage your group to think about what people outside the church will notice about those who are living like Jesus.
- v 6—joy in suffering
- v 8—faith in God
- v 9—a change in priorities and lifestyle, caused by turning from worshipping other things to serving the true God.
- v 10—a conscious, expectant wait for the return of Jesus, who has rescued them and risen from the dead.

● What "report" would your community make about your church? Encourage your group not just to think about what they'd like people to say, or what they themselves would say!

• **What could you do as an individual to make your church's "report" more like the Thessalonians'?** Encourage specific ideas. These might include: looking for opportunities to help neighbours; talking about Christ and church in everyday casual conversation; living a Christ-like life and turning from idols (think about what particular idols your community, and therefore probably you yourselves, are tempted to serve).

• **And collectively?** You might think about: ways to engage with, and serve the community; events which take the church into its local area; how to make services more welcoming, or relevant, or Christ-centred.

EXPLORE MORE
Read Romans 10 v 9-13, Galatians 3 v 8, 13-14, 26-29. How is King Jesus the ultimate fulfilment of God's promise to Abraham of blessing to all nations?
To save time, you can split into small groups and take one passage per group.
Rom 10 v 9-13: Paul announces that people of all nations ("Jew and Gentile") can be blessed with salvation through Jesus Christ.
Gal 3 v 8: Paul explicitly states that the gospel is the fulfilment of God's promise to Abraham about the blessing of the nations.
Gal 3 v 13-14: The blessing is available because Jesus died on the cross in order to satisfy the demands of the law (or "curse") on behalf of lawbreakers, both Jewish and non-Jewish.
Gal 3 v 26-29: Through faith in Jesus (and the public sign of faith, being baptised), we are all in Him, and sons of God, regardless of Jew/Gentile (Greek) background, status, sex. Through Christ, we are all Abraham's children and heirs.

7. How did Solomon show and expand his wealth (v 11-12, v 14-29)?
He showed his wealth by:
• the use of almugwood (v 11-12)
• gold shields (v 16-17) placed in the palace so those who needed to could see them
• the throne (v 18-20) (Notice the "nothing like it" comment and compare with v 10, 12.)
• the use of gold but not silver, showing tremendous wealth (v 21)
He expanded his wealth with:
• trade (v 15, 26-9)
• tribute (v 14-15) ie: payments from neighbouring rulers, recognising his power and to ensure continued friendship with him
• gifts for his wisdom (v 25).

8. 1 Kings 9 v 10 – 10 v 29 shows that Solomon had gifts, wealth, wisdom and influence. What responsibility does he have (look back to 9 v 4-7)? To live God's way, in his heart and actions; not to turn away from God. All he has should be used in service of living like this. You might usefully sum it up as using all God has given him to live for God, to share God's heart priorities, and to rule his people well.

• **How does chapter 10 as a whole suggest he is doing with this responsibility?** In many ways, very well. His kingship is leading others to share God's blessing; and his people are happy and ruled with justice.

9. Read Deuteronomy 17 v 16-17. What is worrying about 1 Kings 10 v 26-29?
God had told His people before they entered the promised land that their kings were not to have a large number of horses; and they were not to get them from Egypt (the nation God had just rescued Israel from). They were

also not to marry "many wives" or they'd be led astray (presumably this refers to foreign wives, whose gods they would end up worshipping, and so reject the true God). Now, Solomon has huge numbers of horses (v 26); and they come from Egypt (v 29). He's not obeying God's commands fully. **Note:** Deut 17 adds that Israel's kings are not to stockpile and hoard large amounts of gold and silver for themselves. It's possible that v 16-17 is hinting that Solomon is falling foul of this command, too—though the writer may simply be wanting to underline the great wealth that the whole kingdom, including Solomon, enjoyed.

• **What does this suggest Solomon is starting to do?** He seems to be beginning to ignore God, and to use his wealth for his own status and enjoyment, rather than to live as God has told him to. Perhaps there is some complacency creeping in. When things are going well, God's people can often begin to compromise in parts of life, presuming that God's blessing will always continue.

10. APPLY: God has given each of His people gifts, wealth, wisdom and influence (though probably not as much as He gave Solomon!). What are our responsibilities when it comes to using these things? Like Solomon, we need to recognise that all that we have and enjoy are God's gifts to us in Christ (see Ephesians 4 v 7-13)—not something that we have earned by our own merit. We need to act accordingly, using what we have been given in the service of Christ. Above all this will mean living out and sharing the gospel, both to build up God's people and as a witness to non-Christians. Get your group to discuss some of the ways in which people can do this in the context of your church/group.

• **What are the dangers of having these things?** The more we have, the more we have the opportunity to become self-reliant and self-serving, seeking our own honour and glory and comfort instead of that of God and His people. Every gift from God is in this sense an opportunity to serve Him, and a dangerous opportunity to reject Him. *And that matters hugely, as we'll see in the next session…*

---

8 **1 Kings 11**
SOLOMON'S FALL

THE BIG IDEA
Solomon's unfaithfulness to God in later life means that he has failed as God's king, and highlights the truth that only Jesus Christ is qualified to rule over God's people.

SUMMARY
1 Kings 11 is probably one of the most

tragic chapters in the Bible. Many will know the story of Solomon well enough to know that it is coming. But it is worth reflecting on what happens here: the one who had the potential to be Israel's greatest king falls—dramatically.

We're told precisely why Solomon falls. Solomon loved foreign women (women he shouldn't have married), and they turned his heart away from God (v 1-4). The one who loved the Lord (3 v 3) becomes, in old age, the one who loved foreign women. Then in verses 5-8 we get the detail of what Solomon did wrong. Note that Solomon falls because of his foreign wives, not because of his wealth—idolatry, rather than greed, is the problem here.

So, not surprisingly, God acts (v 9-13). Notice how God reminds Solomon that He has appeared to him twice (v 9), and yet Solomon has still failed to keep God's explicit command (v 10-11). However, God will show mercy because of David: Solomon himself won't lose the kingdom, and Rehoboam his son won't lose the whole kingdom—one tribe will remain.

The rest of the chapter details how God acts, raising up Hadad (v 14-22) and Rezon (v 23-25) as enemies in the south and the north. But the most significant enemy here is Jeroboam (v 26-40). God takes a capable man (v 28) and uses Him for His own purposes. Notice how Ahijah the prophet's call of Jeroboam, including a promise of blessing for obedience, is very similar to that which David and Solomon received—but notice also how Jeroboam doesn't fully hear and obey the prophetic word, apparently acting on the promise of the ten tribes before Solomon dies.

Finally, this session provides an opportunity to review Solomon's whole life and, in particular, to compare and contrast the tragic fall of history's most privileged king with the perfect kingship of Jesus Christ, and with God's unshakable faithfulness to His word—both His word of judgment and His promise of mercy. There are also lessons to be learned from Solomon's fall into idolatry for our own perseverance in faithfulness to God.

OPTIONAL EXTRA

Find some death-bed quotes and epitaphs on the internet. You could construct a quiz where people have to match famous people with their death-bed quote or epitaph. Or give people a printout, read through them together and discuss how accurately or otherwise each one sums up the life of the famous person who said these words or about whom they were written. Get people to create an epitaph for Solomon, based on what they have learned so far. Towards the end of the session (eg: after Q9) you might like to revisit this and discuss how Solomon's epitaph needs to be changed in the light of what happened towards the end of his life.

GUIDANCE ON QUESTIONS

1. What would you say "idolatry" is? Does it matter? There are no "right answers" to this. Your group may think of idolatry in terms of bowing down to statues, or building a shrine; in which case, ask them if they think idolatry exists in western society. In discussing whether it matters, you might like to ask what the consequence of idolatry is for true faith in God. Q5 will ask your group to use 1 Kings 11 to define what idolatry is and why it matters.

• **How can you work out what you are, or are in danger of, making an idol?** What you can't imagine living without… what you often daydream about… what you get most passionate about… these are all indications of what you are looking to to give you a fulfilling, secure life—that is, an idol (unless it's God, of course!) **Note:** You could choose to use this question after Q5, or with the getting personal box after Q6.

2. What did Solomon do (v 1)? Married lots of "foreign" (ie: not from God's people) wives.

- **Why did that matter (v 2-8)?** God had told His people not to marry foreign people (see Deuteronomy 7 v 1-4, which is one of the passages looked at in Explore More after Q3), and had warned them that this would lead to them loving their made-up gods instead of the true Creator God (v 2).
  This is exactly what happened to Solomon (v 4-5, 7-8). He seems first to have provided the things necessary for his wives to worship their gods, and then to have joined them in it. This seems to have been a gradual process, reaching its climax in Solomon's old age.
  Worshipping other gods meant not treating the LORD as God, who deserves to be followed wholeheartedly (v 6).
  And so Solomon, whose reign had begun with him and his people worshipping at high places in a pagan way (3 v 2-3), and who had helped bring his people to worshipping God at His temple in the way He had commanded (8 v 3-13), ends up building more high places and worshipping other gods there (v 7-8, 5).

3. How does verse 6 sum it up? (You may have already picked this out in Q2, but it's important enough to be repeated.) What Solomon did in worshipping idols as well as God was "evil".

- **What is shocking about the fact that this is *Solomon* that we're reading about?** Solomon has been Israel's greatest king, and the wisest and most discerning man ever. His reign has been the high point of the history of God's people. Under him, God's promises have been fulfilled in a way never before seen: His

people have known peace and happiness in God's land under God's wise, faithful and wealthy king (10 v 6-8); and Israel has been a blessing to other nations as they have come to recognise and praise the LORD (10 v 9). Now, that same king turns his back on the LORD who has so richly blessed him and his people, and worships other gods. It is an absolute tragedy.

EXPLORE MORE
Read Exodus 34 v 11-16 and Deuteronomy 7 v 1-4. Why had God said intermarriage was wrong? Because foreign wives would lead the people astray from the Lord. God's command was not on ethnic grounds, but religious ones. The person (or, in Solomon's case, people) we choose to commit to and live with and know better than anyone else will have a huge influence over our opinions and views and beliefs. God knows this (He created marriage to be this intimate partnership); and so He warned His people that they would stop loving God if they started loving those who reject God and serve other gods.

4. What do God's words in v 9-13 tell us about David and Solomon? God's words in v 9-13 tell us tell us that despite all his wisdom, Solomon has turned away from God, whereas David, who remained faithful to God, is highly esteemed by Him. David was by no means perfect (see 2 Samuel 11); but crucially, he desired in his heart to serve God (v 13, see v 4, 6). Solomon ultimately did not.

- **And about God?** God acts with mercy towards people who serve and love Him, like David. He remembers His promises, even when He is prompted to anger by idolatry. He is a God both of merciful promise-keeping, and just anger at sin.

So here, we see Him finding a way to act in judgment towards Solomon, but also in mercy towards David—He will not completely cut off David's line.

5. APPLY: Using v 1-13, how would you now define:
• **what idolatry is?** It is treating something else as God, replacing God in our hearts with something or someone else. It is loving something else more than God, looking to something other than God to give us our heart's desires (v 2). God deserves 100% devotion and allegiance (v 4, 6); anything that causes us to compromise on that is idolatry.

⊗

• **What are common idols that people in our culture worship to give them what they think they need from life?** We don't tend to bow to statues quite as much—but money, sex, family, marriage, education, wealth, comfort can all become idols for us.

• **why it matters?** Because of what it does to our relationship with God. If we turn away from God, He turns away from us. He is understandably angry when, despite all He has done for us, we decide to love idols instead of Him (v 9). Idolatry leaves us facing judgment and punishment (v 11).

⊗

• **What do you think is the best antidote to idolatry?** We need to fill our minds and hearts with truth about God and how wonderful He is—His faithfulness, mercy, grace, patience, love, justice, fairness. If only Solomon had remembered who the LORD was and how He had blessed him, and then looked

at Chemosh or Molech and what they actually offered (ie: nothing). If only we would look at Jesus Christ—who He is and how He blesses us—we would see how worthless any replacement is, and how stupid it is to replace the Lord with an idol as the thing we love in our heart and serve with our lives.

6. APPLY: How do God's commands to His Old Testament people apply to us as His people today? Read 1 Corinthians 7 v 39 and 2 Corinthians 6 v 14-16. In the same way! Those who are not Christians are not God's people, and the Bible tells us that Christians should not marry them, because we "have nothing in common" with them in terms of our fundamental beliefs about God, the world, and ourselves.

• **How does 1 Kings 11 show that who we are married to is important?** As in Solomon's day, so in ours, our hearts are in great danger of being pulled away from God if we marry someone who at heart is rebelling against the LORD.

Note: This may well be a very difficult subject for some members of your group. You might like to pick one or more of the following extra questions:

⊗

• **Why do you think we so often ignore this command as Christians today?** Allow your group to suggest ideas. Perhaps it is because we think we know better than God: that we can serve Him and be married to someone who is serving an idol. Or, because we think we need more than God—so we marry someone even though God tells us not to (in which case, we've made our spouse themselves an idol). Or often, it's because our churches are silent on this matter, and so we get married to someone who makes us happy and looks after us, without thinking about how it will impact our faith in Christ.

- **Read 1 Corinthians 7 v 12-13. What does God say about a situation in which a Christian and non-Christian are already married?** They should stay married, as long as their partner is willing to live with them while they follow Christ and put Him first. For people who are in this situation (for whatever reason), it's better not to regret what has already happened, but to be aware of the constant pull to compromise on how they live for God. Verse 16 reminds us that a Christian's main hope in this situation will be that their husband or wife is saved by turning to Christ (see also 1 Peter 3 v 1-2)—but there's no guarantee this will happen.

- **Read 1 Corinthians 7 v 7-8, 32-35. How should we approach the issue of being single when we'd rather not be?** All we need in life is found in our relationship with Christ, and serving Him; if He has decided for the time being to give us single status to use to serve Him, then we must trust that His plan for us is right). This is really not easy. But through God's grace and help, many single Christians have lived, and felt that they have been living, fulfilling lives as they serve Him in His world.

7. God had given faithful Solomon "rest on every side, and … no adversary" (5 v 4). How is this blessing withdrawn (v 14-25)?
- God raises up an adversary, Hadad (v 14). Hadad is married to one of Pharaoh's daughters (v 19), just as Solomon is (3 v 1), neutralising a key alliance of his.

- God also raises up Rezon (v 23)—and both now cause Solomon trouble (v 25).

We see here that God acts to discipline those who turn away from Him—He has raised up these men "against Solomon" (v 14, 23). This is what God promised to David that He would do (see 2 Samuel 7 v 14).

8. How does God fulfil His promise of verses 11-13 (v 26-40)? You might want to recap what God had said would happen because of Solomon's disobedience and idolatry:
- He would lose his kingdom to someone who had worked for him (v 11)
- This would happen after Solomon's death, because he was the son of David, who had been obedient (v 12). Our reaction may be that this meant Solomon didn't suffer for his own sin, but one of the greatest duties of a monarch was to secure his kingdom for his son to take his place, and Solomon had to live out his days knowing that he could not do this.
- A small part of the kingdom would be left in the hands of David's line (v13).

In verse 26, we meet Jeroboam, "one of Solomon's officials" (v 26). The LORD speaks to him through Ahijah the prophet (v 29-30), saying:
- He will be given ten tribes of Israel to rule over (v 31).
- One tribe, Judah, will be left to Solomon's son (v 34-36).

Notice that Solomon, though he tries, cannot get rid of Jeroboam (v 40).

- **What hope is left for David's line?** Solomon's son will be king over one tribe (v 36) and rule Jerusalem, the site of the LORD's temple. Though God will judge David's descendants because of Solomon's sin (v 39—which Solomon's descendants followed Solomon in, see for instance 14 v 21-24, 15 v 1-3), this won't go on for ever. We are left waiting for a King in David and Solomon's line who will obey God and be exalted, rather than one who disobeys God and is judged.

9. Verse 43 marks the end of King Solomon's remarkable reign. On the graph below, draw a curve of how things have gone for God's people under Solomon's rule. See bottom of page. Of course, our line is just an indication—feel free to disagree!

10. APPLY: How do these verses both challenge and comfort us as we reflect on:
• **who God is?** *Challenge:* we need to recognise the consistency of God's character, and therefore the reality of judgment—God will keep the promises that He has made. For Christians that means He will keep the promises that He has made in His Son—Jesus is the only way to the Father—but that also means

that those who deny Jesus will suffer eternity under His judgment.
Comfort: We, His people, can draw comfort from knowing God is sovereign— we can rely on and trust in Him, knowing that He will keep His promises. Whatever comes our way, God is in control.

• **what humans (even Solomon) are like?**
Challenge: even the best and most blessed and privileged of us are sinners, who disobey God, and who worship things other than God, and so who deserve judgment as Solomon did.
Comfort: God continues to deal with sinful humanity. Our sin does not surprise Him, nor does it derail His plans. And the judgment on sin is "not for ever" (v 39).

11. APPLY: How does the best of Solomon's rule and kingdom leave us aching for the establishment of Jesus Christ's rule and kingdom? Solomon's early rule was with wisdom and justice. His kingdom was blessed, peaceful, wealthy and contented. To live in it was wonderful—and since this was just a foretaste of Jesus'

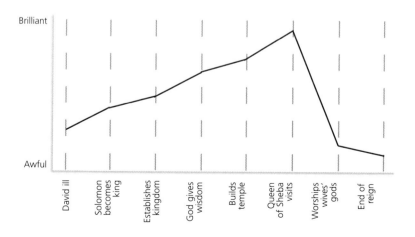

kingdom, reading about it should make us long for the day when Christ returns and His kingdom fills the whole earth.

- **How does the worst of Solomon's rule and kingdom leave us aching too?!**

  The end of Solomon's rule was wrecked by his disobedience and idolatry. And so his kingdom was divided, and soon God's people followed their kings into idolatry (see 14 v 22-24). Solomon's downfall leaves us rejoicing that we have a King who never turned away from God, and whose kingdom is eternal. And as we see Solomon in ourselves, in our decisions and flaws (and those around us in our family or church), we rejoice all the more that we won't always be like this: one day we'll be perfected as we live with our perfect King.

Note: Solomon's failure to be the faithful king that God required should not be seen as God's first plan falling apart, and which meant He needed to come up with a second plan—Jesus Christ. God's plan was always to send Jesus Christ into our world. But before He did so, He set out to show humanity that all the ways in which men try to deal with the problem of sin and to be reconciled with God will fail (see for example Hebrews 8), so that we would recognise that Jesus Christ is our only hope. Solomon's reign was part of that process, showing that the greatest of merely human kings, even when blessed so abundantly by God, cannot live as God commands, nor lead God's people as God requires. We need a perfect king— we need Jesus!

Good Book Guides
The growing range

thegoodbook
COMPANY

BIBLICAL | RELEVANT | ACCESSIBLE

At The Good Book Company, we are dedicated to helping Christians and local churches grow. We believe that God's growth process always starts with hearing clearly what he has said to us through his timeless word—the Bible.

Ever since we opened our doors in 1991, we have been striving to produce resources that honor God in the way the Bible is used. We have grown to become an international provider of user-friendly resources to the Christian community, with believers of all backgrounds and denominations using our Bible studies, books, evangelistic resources, DVD-based courses, and training events.

We want to equip ordinary Christians to live for Christ day by day, and churches to grow in their knowledge of God, their love for one another, and the effectiveness of their outreach.

Call us for a discussion of your needs or visit one of our local websites for more information on the resources and services we provide.

Your friends at The Good Book Company

NORTH AMERICA   thegoodbook.com   866 244 2165
UK & EUROPE   thegoodbook.co.uk   0333 123 0880
AUSTRALIA   thegoodbook.com.au   (02) 9564 3555
NEW ZEALAND   thegoodbook.co.nz

  WWW.CHRISTIANITYEXPLORED.ORG
Our partner site is a great place for those exploring the Christian faith, with a clear explanation of the good news, powerful testimonies and answers to difficult questions.